MARION ETTLINGER

About the Author

DENIS JOHNSON is playwright in residence for the Campo Santo theater company at San Francisco's Intersection for the Arts. He is the author of several books of fiction and verse, as well as a collection of articles. His plays have been produced in San Francisco and New York. *Hellhound on My Trail* received a 2000 San Francisco Bay Area Theatre Critics Circle Outstanding Achievement Award for Original Script.

SHOPPERS

ALSO BY DENIS JOHNSON

Seek

The Name of the World

Already Dead

Jesus' Son

Fiskadoro

The Stars at Noon

Resuscitation of a Hanged Man

Angels

The Throne of the Third Heaven of the Nations
Millennium General Assembly

SHOPPERS

TWO PLAYS

DENIS JOHNSON

Perennial

An Imprint of HarperCollins*Publishers*

Hellhound on My Trail was previously published in *McSweeney's*.

Shoppers Carried by Escalators into the Flames was developed
with assistance from Robert Redford's Sundance Theater Lab.
The author is most grateful.

HarperCollins books may be purchased for educational,
business, or sales promotional use. For information please write:
Special Markets Department, HarperCollins Publishers Inc.,
10 East 53rd Street, New York, NY 10022.

FIRST EDITION

Designed by Jennifer Ann Daddio

Library of Congress Cataloging-in-Publication Data

Johnson, Denis.
[Hellhound on my trail]
Shoppers : two plays / by Denis Johnson.
p.   cm.
Contents: Hellhound on my trail—Shoppers
carried by escalators into the flames.
ISBN 0-06-093440-9 (alk. paper)
I. Johnson, Denis. Shoppers carried by escalators into
the flames. II. Title: Shoppers carried by escalators into
the flames. III. Title.
PS3560.O3745 H45 2002
813'.54—dc21
2001051933

02 03 04 05 06 WB/RRD 10 9 8 7 6 5 4 3 2 1

This volume is dedicated with immense gratitude to

SEAN SAN JOSE

HELLHOUND ON MY TRAIL

A DRAMA IN THREE PARTS

Hellhound on My Trail was written for Campo Santo + Intersection and premiered at Intersection for the Arts (Deborah Cullinan, executive director) in San Francisco, California, on July 26, 2000.

Produced by Campo Santo (James Faerron, Margo Hall, Sean San Jose, Luis Saguar, Michael Torres, Drew Yerys; Denis Johnson: playwright in residence)

Cast

MARIGOLD: Alexis Lezin
MRS. MAY: Anne Darragh
JACK TOAST: Michael Torres
KATE WENDELL: Delia MacDougall
CASS: Sean San Jose
SALAZAR: Brian Keith Russell

Original musical score by Marcus Shelby

Vocals by Scheherazade Stone

Designed by Jim Cave, Suzanne Castillo,
James Faerron, and Drew Yerys

Directed by Val Hendrickson

A workshop production of *Hellhound on My Trail* was staged in September-October 2001, by the Atlantic Theater Company (Neil Pepe, artistic director; Hillary Hinkel, managing director) in New York City.

Cast

MARIGOLD: Molly Powell
MRS. MAY: Jennifer Regan
KATE WENDELL: Sharon Scruggs
JACK TOAST: Kevin Hurley
CASS: Bill Dawes
SALAZAR: Jim Frangione

Directed by David Levine

1. An Exploration of the Colorado River

MARIGOLD: A woman in her late twenties
MRS. MAY: A woman in her late forties

Scene: An office in Houston

2. Head Rolling and Rolling

KATE WENDELL: A woman in her thirties
JACK TOAST: A man in his forties

Scene: A coffee shop in Houston

3. Hellhound on My Trail

CASS: A man just past thirty
SALAZAR: A man in his forties

Scene: A motel room fifty miles outside Houston

Sets and lighting should be simple and true-to-life; no music except as indicated.

1. An Exploration of the Colorado River

MRS. MAY's *office: At stage left a large desk and swivel chair, fronted by a comfortable chair for visitors. Across the space at right, a couch and a large chair separated by a low table. Looks like a cross between an office and a waiting room.*

Upstage, a wall with venetian blinds over a window.

Morning outside.

Alone in the room, MARIGOLD CASSANDRA *sits on the couch. Late twenties. Business suit.*

She looks at magazines from a stack on the low table. Tosses one aside, and it slides off the table onto the floor. Crosses and uncrosses her legs, etc.

She opens her purse, rummages distractedly. Comes up with a bottle of pills. Pause. Unscrews the cap and downs one. Pause. Reaches in her mouth and takes it out. Pause. Puts it back in her mouth, clamped by her front teeth.

Hunts in her purse again. Finds a little airline liquor bottle and quickly unscrews its cap and washes down the pill with a swallow.

MARIGOLD: Oh. Jesus Christ.

Gets a breath spray from her purse and opens wide and hits her larynx. Finds some gum in her purse. Unwraps and chews it. Tosses the wrapper into the purse. Stares down into it.

Pause. She spits the gum into the purse.

She takes another pill, rapidly repeating the whole process, emptying the tiny jug and tossing it into the purse. And then more breathspray. More gum. She sighs.

Pause.

The door opens a crack. A woman peeks in and smiles: MRS. MAY, *late forties, in a black dress with white borders, the senior citizen look. She knocks tentatively and enters with a slightly hunched, apologetic air—leaves the door ajar behind her. She looks around, adjusts the blinds to make more light. Gathers magazines into stacks, picking up the one on the floor. She talks softly, as if in deference to people working in nearby offices.*

MRS. MAY: Were you looking at this one?

MARIGOLD: No. Yes. But not now. (*Pause.*) I didn't expect magazines! (*Pause.*) Is this a waiting room? Is there an inner office?

MRS. MAY: Oh, this is the inner office. I'll take these old ones home . . . Unless you—?

MARIGOLD: No. Thanks.

MRS. MAY: This one's recent. (*Showing it.*) How did they get that?

MARIGOLD: Horrible.

MRS. MAY: He was right *in* the fire. Snapping pictures . . . Look at that. It looks like Iwo Jima, doesn't it, with the flag, only they're being crushed.

Pause. MARIGOLD, *looking, gasps in polite appreciation.*

MRS. MAY: Carried by escalators into the flames . . . (*Pause.*) Did you see the news on TV when it, after they—

MARIGOLD: Horrible. Wasn't it more than eighty—

MRS. MAY: They were laid out like shish kebab in the parking lot . . . And it was raining. And the steam was rising off the corpses in the rain.

MARIGOLD: I don't remember that.

MRS. MAY: Don't you?

MARIGOLD: Not—isn't the sun—were these pictures taken that day? Because it seems sunny—

MRS. MAY: —it seems sunny—

MARIGOLD: It does.

MRS. MAY: I probably misremembered. Every time you turn on the TV. Don't you agree, Ms. Cassandra? All the corpses blur together. (*Pause.*) I'm sorry—

MARIGOLD: No. I just got startled. My name— You knew. I didn't think— Well, perhaps I should ask: Are you— (*Pause.* MRS. MAY *is leaning close to her.*) Do I— (MARIGOLD *leans back.*) —smell funny? I mean . . . For instance is my perfume all right?

MRS. MAY: Wow. You *are* nervous!

MARIGOLD: They flew me from Dallas.

MRS. MAY: It's a hundred and *one* in Dallas. Already this morning!

MARIGOLD: That's— I mean, I can believe it. It's terrible there. Really hot. All the time. (*Pause.*) Was it a special news item? Or do you—you know, maybe you have some relatives— (MRS. MAY *is fanning the air in front of her face.*) Are you sure you don't—if you whiff sort of— (MARIGOLD *turns away, finds her breath mist.*)

MRS. MAY (*Standing, arranging things on the desk*): Yes. (*Pause.*) It was a special news item. Hottest place in the USA. Hotter than Phoenix. Hotter than Yuma. Oh, they'll catch up by noon. They're in the desert and the temperature drops off when the sun goes down. But Dallas didn't cool off at all last night . . . It's down around ninety here in Houston.

Meanwhile, MARIGOLD *inhales a puff of freshener, gets the device back in her purse, turns to find* MRS. MAY *seated comfortably behind the desk.*

MARIGOLD: When do you think—

Pause.

MARIGOLD'S *jaw drops.*

Pause.

MARIGOLD: I feel like my plane crashed and I'm dead.

Pause.

MRS. MAY: I'm sorry . . . Were you about to ask—?

Pause.

MARIGOLD: I was about to ask when you thought you'd get here.

MRS. MAY: But I'm here.

Pause.

MARIGOLD: I know. How do you do, Mrs. May?

MRS. MAY *gestures.* MARIGOLD *sits in the chair before the desk.*

Pause.

MRS. MAY: I do smell liquor. Is it you?

MARIGOLD: No. Of course not.

Pause.

MARIGOLD: It's probably just mouthwash.

Pause.

MARIGOLD *opens her mouth to speak, changes her mind.*

Pause.

MRS. MAY: Were you about to speak?

MARIGOLD: Yes.

Pause.

MRS. MAY: And . . . ?

MARIGOLD: I thought better of it.

Pause.

MRS. MAY: Marigold?

MARIGOLD: Yes.

MRS. MAY: May I call you Marigold?

MARIGOLD: Certainly. I like my name. Please do.

MRS. MAY: Marigold . . .

Pause.

Would you like to begin by making a statement in your own words?

MARIGOLD: I'm sorry, no.

MRS. MAY: All right.

MARIGOLD: I'm happy to address any questions I can answer briefly. I'm completely new to this—procedure. I have no idea what the procedure *is* or even if this is, I mean actually, a procedure, something with a pre-set . . . I'll tell you this much. I found myself on the merry-go-round where the gold ring grabs *you*. You just, we just, you sit around waiting for the shadow to fall on you . . . When I was a girl at home, we had—back in Ukiah—in California   I kept chickens. Every once in a while a hawk'll get one. They come ramming out of the clouds full speed and knock a chicken's head off. Dig out a few handfuls of breast and adios. I can't see how a rambling monologue . . . Uh—beyond this admittedly extensive depiction of the situation . . . (*Pause.*) District Nine as the Chicken Coop of Doom . . .

Pause.

MRS. MAY: You've been with Agriculture for—five years?

MARIGOLD: And about seven months. Five years and seven months.

MRS. MAY: You're currently Level Four. Have I got that right?

MARIGOLD: Right. Yes. Administrative and Field Coordinator, Second Class. Yes.

MRS. MAY: At the time of the Kernwood Farms investigation—that is, the second investigation, the one in which you took part—

MARIGOLD: I was Acting AFC, First Class. That was temporary. It was understood at the outset to be temporary.

MRS. MAY: All right. A general question. Happy with the work?

MARIGOLD: Uh. No. (*Pause.*) I mean, for the last couple of years I've just been waiting for this part to be over with.

MRS. MAY: And—more generally than that? Overall?

MARIGOLD: Yes. Very definitely. I travel, I meet new people . . . I'm always forced to confront new tasks . . . I'm always learning. I guess in some ways that's because we make everything we do, you know—a little harder than it has to be.

MRS. MAY: So sometimes you're disillusioned.

MARIGOLD: No, no. It's just the nature of . . . In a *bureaucracy*—

MRS. MAY: You're not disillusioned by the work. Only by its nature.

MARIGOLD: No, of course not, but I . . . But what do we *do*? We inspect food. I mean—haven't human beings sort of— been inspecting whatever goes in their mouths since—you know—they couldn't have invented the *wheel* if they couldn't keep from killing themselves with stuff they ate . . . I mean in a way . . . we're less developed than cave-dwellers . . .

MRS. MAY: Marigold.

MARIGOLD: Yes.

MRS. MAY: You're being open with me, and I'd like to be the same.

MARIGOLD: Yes.

MR. MAY: Well, all right. It's this. My feelings are hurt.

MARIGOLD: Why—

MRS. MAY: Why are my feelings hurt?

MARIGOLD: Yes.

Pause.

MRS. MAY: Because I'm realizing you have no appreciation for the purity of what I do. (*Pause.*) I don't inspect food. I have no interest in what you do. Or what the Department does. None whatsoever. Or in anything that goes on outside this room. Or ever will. Or ever has gone on. All I am I dedicate to what we're doing now.

MARIGOLD: And—what is that?

MRS. MAY: I am interrogating you.

Pause. A really long one.

Everything I've done since we found ourselves together here a few minutes ago has been designed to further the process. The light is neither intense nor dim. It is neutral. Do you see? The chair is comfortable, but it doesn't invite you to doze off. Nothing around you here is intended to intimidate . . . When I showed you the pictures in the newsmagazine I meant to posit a world which we have left and to which we don't really wish to return, do we?—not now, not while we have this process all around us . . . A world of charred bodies. A history that is really entirely out of our control. Whereas here in the Department things are actually within our grasp: if we adopt procedures, carry them out, all of that. It seems so boring, doesn't it? But it's a universe actually under our control. An elaborate collaboration. Government really doesn't govern anything, does it? But it can attempt to govern itself. It's possible it may, from time to time, succeed. But. The attempt doesn't consist of *trying*. We don't profit by an attitude of *trying*.

A long pause.

You're doing awfully well at remaining quiet.

Pause.

MARIGOLD: Thank you.

Pause.

MRS. MAY: At not volunteering information.

Pause.

MARIGOLD: Thank you.

Pause.

MRS. MAY: I want to suggest an attitude for us both to take, Ms. Cassandra. May I do that? Marigold?

MARIGOLD: Of course.

MRS. MAY: Let me read you a passage from a journal. Do you know who John Wesley Powell was?

MARIGOLD: No, I'm afraid not.

MRS. MAY: Mr. Powell was an explorer. His party were the first white people to navigate the Colorado River in the early nineteenth century. May I read you this paragraph from his journal?

Pause. MARIGOLD *shrugs.*

MRS. MAY (*reading*): "The canyon is much narrower than any we have seen. With difficulty we manage our boats. They spin about from side to side, and we know not where we are going, and find it impossible to keep them headed down the stream. At first, this causes us great alarm, but we soon find there is but little danger, and there is a general movement of progression down the river, to which this whirling is but an adjunct; and it is the merry mood of the river to dance through this deep dark gorge . . ."

Pause.

MARIGOLD: Well, all right. (*Pause.*) I'm guessing you want me to cooperate like a lost soul on a raft in a raging river. (*Brighter:*) That sort of reminds me—or more sort of *surrender*. But speaking of the Colorado—

MRS. MAY: What was the basic function—(MARIGOLD *is silenced*)—or the goal, as you understood it, of Team One?

Pause.

Did something remind you of something did you say?

MARIGOLD: . . . It was . . . No. Nothing. Sorry.

MRS. MAY: All right. I'll repeat . . . What was the basic function, or the goal, as you understood it, of Team One?

MARIGOLD: I was happy when I got Team One.

MRS. MAY: That doesn't answer my inquiry.

MARIGOLD: I was happy for reasons that turned out to be bad things. Team One sounded primary. Top Team. It was really only equal to any other, and we were all clear about that, but it *felt* more in the spotlight. "We're number one." And now it gets more of the heat.

MRS. MAY: Team One gets no heat whatsoever, Marigold. The chapter is closed . . . We're here for a back-and-forth exchange. I'm only picking Team One as a starting point for this exchange . . .

And what was the mission of Team One?

MARIGOLD: Can I ask you something? Why do you want to know about Team One if you have no interest in what we do? As you say.

Pause.

MRS. MAY: Marigold . . . I'm asking the questions.

Pause.

MARIGOLD: We were in charge of the jam.

MRS. MAY: And ultimately the jam got not only the spotlight, but the cameras, didn't it? And the notoriety.

MARIGOLD: Yes, ma'am, it did. The jam was not the place to be.

(Pause. MRS. MAY *relaxes. A sense of shifting gears: we're cruising now.)*

MRS. MAY: Were you satisfied, inititially, with the plan as outlined?

MARIGOLD: Yes, I was. We were all very excited, all the teams, but particularly those of us on Team One, because we had the jam, and that made us one of the two link teams with the Food and Drug people. *(Pause.)* Nobody realized we didn't actually have a plan. We had goals. We had procedures. We had the teams. But that didn't add up to an actual step-by-step. *(Pause.)* And since Kernwood Farms grows all the food it cans *except* the fruit, our team was scrutinizing the part of their operation involving commerce with orchards, transport of fresh produce, all of that. The jam. And I had the top spot on the Jam Team.

MRS. MAY: Your team were you; Jones; Michaels; Delacorte; Tooey. That is, Michaels known as Michaels One.

MARIGOLD: Jones—

MRS. MAY: And Jones One.

MARIGOLD: Yes.

MRS. MAY: And Alan Tooey.

MARIGOLD: Here we go.

MRS. MAY (*sympathetically*): Didn't you find yourself sometimes alone with any of your team, sometimes under
extreme pressure as the investigation became nightmarish?

MARIGOLD: Yes. And I wish you'd get to the question I know
you're going to ask, so I can deny it ever happened.

MRS. MAY: Did you invite Alan Tooey to apply jam to your
private places and lick it away?

MARIGOLD: Never. Not even close. Alan Tooey is psychotic.

MRS. MAY: Well then.

MARIGOLD: You're all loony.

MRS. MAY: That question is behind us.

MARIGOLD: Are you writing this down?

MRS. MAY: No. As you see.

MARIGOLD: Oh.

MRS. MAY: It's being recorded.

MARIGOLD (*glancing around*): Fine.

MRS. MAY: Because tone of voice is often so important. With-out it, a remark can sound absurd, or damning, when it's really neither one. Do you see?

MARIGOLD: I've seen that everything is either absurd or damning, yes, ma'am.

Pause.

So my outburst will be perfectly preserved. In a little bureaucratic jar of jam.

MRS. MAY: I welcome your outbursts. I think of them as explosions of truth . . . Marigold, facts aren't truth. Only when a fact has been interpreted by a desiring mind and colored by emotion does it become truth.

MARIGOLD: You've been at this work a long, long time.

MRS. MAY: Do you understand what I'm saying? When I tell you I'm not interested in what you do, I'm actually being even more radical than that might sound. I'm telling you I'm completely uninterested in the facts. This inquiry is your chance to be understood.

MARIGOLD: I appreciate that.

MRS. MAY: No, you don't really. You're just being polite.

MARIGOLD: Okay. So—then, shove it!

MRS. MAY *laughs. Sobers. Pause.*

MRS. MAY: When I asked you the question you wanted me to ask concerning you and Mr. Alan Tooey—I asked you to say yes or no to a report that claimed to be factual.

MARIGOLD: I understand that. And it never happened.

MRS. MAY: Well, I would hope that even if it *had* happened, you would deny it. I hope that in order to be *truthful,* you would deny the facts . . . Because a statement of the bare facts can be an awful lie, can't it?

Pause.

MARIGOLD: Those are not the facts.

MRS. MAY *opens her drawer and produces three sheets of letter-size paper, laying them out side by side in front of* MARIGOLD. MARIGOLD *doesn't move a muscle.*

MRS. MAY: This is the two-paragraph statement submitted by Alan Tooey. You've seen it?

MARIGOLD: I've seen it. I've got a copy in my purse.

MRS. MAY: Mr. Tooey made the statement and signed it. You see there's a line for your signature also.

MARIGOLD: I'll sign. Do you think I care anymore?

MRS. MAY: About this? I hope you don't. I certainly don't.

MARIGOLD: I don't. I have nothing but contempt for what's happening here.

MRS. MAY: *I* have more contempt for these statements than I would have for excrement.

MARIGOLD: I need some sort of representative. I should have asked for a representative.

MRS. MAY: You're putting me on.

MARIGOLD: Of course not.

MRS. MAY: Deceiving me.

MARIGOLD: I just want a representative.

MRS. MAY: Marigold, I think you got up this morning, knocked back a double at Charlie's Time-out Lounge across the street, and floated in here without any clear ideas about anything.

MARIGOLD: I am formally asking for—

MRS. MAY: *I* am your representative.

Pause.

Marigold, I am the Ombudsperson for Human Resources for the Southwestern Region. *I* take your case to *them.* If necessary in order to demonstrate my contempt for this statement of facts I will douse myself with gasoline and set myself afire in their offices. You and I—we are an emotional aristocracy. Everything that is being done here is beneath us. I support you in signing this statement as a gesture underlining its complete absurdity.

Pause. Just as MARIGOLD *leans forward and takes a breath to speak . . .*

Since the jam fiasco you've been placed under Katherine Wendell, who transferred temporarily from District Five. You understand the purpose of Kate Wendell's temporary assignment.

MARIGOLD: Kate Wendell is among us to collect scalps.

MRS. MAY: Precisely. That is what she does. She is now in the process of sawing yours from your skull. She's brought a series of flagrantly silly actions against you in the last eighteen months. This is the latest, putting you up for suspension while Human Resources rejuvenates this ancient allegation. As if they understood the atmosphere of that night, the way it felt to be *you,* a million miles from the people judging all this, who know nothing of how it feels, how it tastes in your mouth, the chaos of a night like the one you endured at Kernwood Farms. Do you mind if I say something that might be misinterpreted outside this room? . . . You are lovely, and alone.

Pause. MARIGOLD *shrugs helplessly.*

So very much like—that night, that young girl, the black factory girl, wasn't she lovely?

MARIGOLD: Yes.

MRS. MAY: So lovely and so alone. When she sang the National Anthem.

MARIGOLD: I know. Of course, I know, believe me.

MRS. MAY: There are some things that make you understand history is being made. I mean that every moment is history. That is what I meant by steam rising off the corpses in the rain. Even it if never happened, do you see . . .

MARIGOLD: I'm—no. I'm not sure I—but of course I remember Tanya Cruz in her lab-coat thing singing "The Star Spangled Banner." Believe me—with her hair net—

MRS. MAY: A sixteen-year old black child sings "O say can you see!" in a jam factory, and the United States Department of Agriculture trembles to its roots—

MARIGOLD (overlapping): —I knew things would never be the same in my little life . . . I could feel a dozen United States Senators scrambling for position to ream us all in the name of Tanya Cruz. She was cute as a bug, and she could sing. Is that history?

MRS. MAY (overlapping): —history. Whether it happened or not.

MARIGOLD: Oh, it happened.

MRS. MAY: But it had the tenor of emotion. It vibrated with life, it didn't lie there *deceased,* Marigold, like a *fact,* do you see, it *was* "nothing" and it *meant* "something."

Pause.

Where were you at that moment? In Washington? For the hearings?

MARIGOLD: No. I was there that night. I didn't see the tape till later, like everybody else.

MRS. MAY: Could you hear her singing?

MARIGOLD: No, the seventeen girls were cut off from us, we had no visual, no audio. The FDA people had a phone hookup, but the girls had stopped answering. It was like they were hostages in there, but nobody was holding them. They could have walked out any time they wanted. We didn't know they had a camcorder.

MRS. MAY: It was incredibly hot that night. In the upper nineties, wasn't it?

MARIGOLD: Yes.

MRS. MAY: That's partly what I meant by pressure, when I asked if you didn't find yourself under pressure, alone with a fellow worker—you realize I mean Tooey—

MARIGOLD: It was hot, yes, muggy, and the frogs were squawking and the bugs were screaming. Big patches of dark, the fields were like vast dark craters, and then other places with glaring lights, TV crews, a couple of food service trucks—throbbing generators—exhaust off the generators— and a sweet smell—some kind of blossom . . .

MRS. MAY: Throbbing generators.

Pause.

MARIGOLD: Sitting in the car, sweating. If we cracked the window for air, the skeeters swarmed in. Keep the skeeters out, it was like a steam cooker in there. The Senate hearings were two thousand miles away. Texas all around us. Louisiana over there about sixty miles. Over in that direction you could feel the continent turning to mush. To swamp. You could feel ghosts with malaria wandering around. Old spells, brown bones, voodoo curses. Like we were sitting on a little saucer of earth that had been cut away underneath us, and here we are, floating in all of this red darkness that was completely real, but the *issue,* the goals, the plan, the strategy, the Department of Agriculture—that was . . . a comic book, a dream. Somebody made it up. I'm holding this jar of Kernwood Farms jam and it could've been full of secret voodoo fetuses. I mean it was scary and ridiculous—a jar full of Looziana madness, we'd opened it and it was all over us . . .

MRS. MAY: And you couldn't respond to that sense of unreality, you couldn't pay homage to that absurdity and that fear simply by saying, "Everything seems so crazy!" Holding this ridiculous jar of jam. Those seventeen girls in there trapped for the third day, a simple inspection turned into a movie, into the Alamo—you picked up this jar of jam in the dark and said—

MARIGOLD: Exactly! I said, hey, Alan, you wanna throw this on my tits and lick it off?

MRS. MAY: It was a poem!

MARIGOLD: It *was*.

MRS. MAY (*singing softly, clearly, with feeling*): "Oh, say can you
   see by the dawn's early light, what so proudly we hailed, at
   the twi-light's last gleaming?"

Pause.
   Weeping silently, MARIGOLD *lifts the pen and signs one of the*
forms. Pause: both women quite still except that MARIGOLD *shudders*
slightly, sobbing without sound. She signs a second copy.
   She positions the third copy before her.
   Phone rings. Both women motionless. Once, twice.

MRS. MAY *picks up phone, cutting off third ring.*

MRS. MAY: Bruce. (*Closes her eyes and takes the phone away from*
   her head. Pause. Puts the phone back to her ear. Opens her eyes.)
   What is the meaning of this. (*Pause. She grows alert.*) All
   right. (*Pause.*) George . . . (*Long pause.*) Georgina! Is this—?
   (*Pause.*) Well, obviously! But is it *your* nonsense, is it April
   Fool's—she asked respectfully. (*Pause.*) No. Thank you. Once
   was fine. (*Pause.*) Yes, I'd better, of course—Georgina, I
   think you've addled me! (*Peers at fax machine.*) Eight-eight-
   eight, two hundred, twelve hundred. (*Pause.*) First thing
   after lunch. (*Pause.*) Oh, Georgina! Each time a citizen writes
   a letter do we have to jump onto planes and float miles in the
   air and go into rooms to say things we could say on the
   phone? (*Pause. Laughs desperately.*) Let's—after lunch, and
   we'll decide. All right? Please? Respectfully. Please. (*Pause.*)
   Fine. It's right here beside me . . . Bye, George.

Hangs up. She studies MARIGOLD.
  Pause.

MRS. MAY: What have you done?

MARIGOLD: Me?

MRS. MAY: What has your husband done?

MARIGOLD: Who?

MRS. MAY: Mr. Cassandra?

MARIGOLD: I'm not married.

MRS. MAY: Then Mr. Cassandra is—

MARIGOLD: I guess my—what is his first name?

MRS. MAY: Who?

MARIGOLD: My brother.

MRS. MAY: You've misplaced your brother's first name?

MARIGOLD: I have three brothers, if it's my brother. But if it
  isn't Mark or Luke or John, then I don't know.

MRS. MAY: What.

MARIGOLD: Who it *is*.

Pause.

MRS. MAY: And you're aware of what your brother has done.

MARIGOLD: Is it Mark?

MRS. MAY: And you're aware of what he's done, but you won't say clearly that it's your brother who's undertaking this . . . mischief. Because that's all it is.

MARIGOLD: Good. Okay. Because if you told me Cass was up a tall building with an arsenal, I'd believe it. Everybody calls him Cass. My brother Mark.

MRS. MAY: He doesn't have an arsenal.

Pause.

MARIGOLD: Does he have a gun?

MRS. MAY: You tell me. What sort of firepower do *you* think we're talking about?

MARIGOLD *gets up, asserting herself very reluctantly . . .*

MARIGOLD: I should—where is this happening? I don't even know what town he lives in! I've gotta—maybe I should be there.

MRS. MAY: There are people who handle these matters.

MARIGOLD: But—

MRS. MAY: Ms. Cassandra. Marigold. Right now you're bringing an incredible energy into this room. You've torn the roof off and—*money* is pouring in. So I'm a little reluctant to bring you back to earth.

MARIGOLD: I want to get back to earth!

MRS. MAY: Sometimes it isn't—what I allow to invigorate me isn't clean. I think I'm destroying myself.

MARIGOLD: GODDAMN YOU.

Pause.

MRS. MAY: A Mark Cassandra has sent a letter to the National Director of Human Resources.

Pause.

MARIGOLD: That's all.

MRS. MAY: It's plenty.

MARIGOLD: I'd like to ask a question. (*Pause.*) When you came in here you appeared to be something like a receptionist or almost the cleaning lady, and then it turned out you're not, you're the troubleshooter for Regional Human Resources, but isn't it possible you're really not the troubleshooter for Regional Human Resources but actually really in fact the FUCKING CLEANING LADY? Because you are insane. And it's easier to figure hey, an insane cleaning lady, than to think wow, the Human Resources Ombudsperson for the Southwest Region is a sadistic homosexual maniac.

A long, long pause. They start out staring each other down and then their eyes drift away.

The fax machine starts up and emits a document. This process absorbs the two of them as they watch it from beginning to end.

Pause.

MRS. MAY: The text of your brother's letter has arrived. Oh, a personal touch. (*Shows it.*) Handwritten. (*Reads:*) "Dear Director Jameson. Out of a family pretty well running wild all over Texas and California and the entire United States, which is the Cassandra family, my sister is the only good one. Her name is Marigold Cassandra. The only good Cassandra ever born. This is to bring your attention to the following facts:" (*Pause. She reads on, silently.*) Oh—look here. Down at the bottom. (*She leans across the desk with the letter.*) Look at those two words. Would you read those two words? Aloud, please?

MARIGOLD: No.

MRS. MAY (*reading*): "First. Number One: A person called Kate Wendell was made my sister's boss. Started in riding my sister Marigold and hasn't let up since, which is well over a year of unjustified bullshit. Number Two. Just look in the files. It's complete and utter chickenshit the stuff this woman Kate Wendell finds to complain about. Third. This woman is a lesbian after my sister. Making passes and remarks and threats. I'm calling sexual harrassment. Number Four. Everything I'm telling you adds up that Kate Wendell is the one to be charged with something, not Marigold Cassandra.

"I am a ripper and runner and I sure know the stink off

another skunk like me when I get up next to one. And that about covers Ms. Kate Wendell.

"My sister has a tough enough job. Which she is tough enough to get it done. But she is still that most tendermost creature, a human. Do not fail her by keeping her at the mercy of a"—the mercy of a—what. (*Pause.*) Just let me hear you read those two words out loud.

Pause. MARIGOLD *is stone.*

MRS. MAY: But you did read them to yourself silently. (*Pause.*) And you've already said them out loud once today. You've read them and you've said them. I'm just asking you to do it once more.

Pause. MRS. MAY *reaches into her desk, takes out a small recorder, holds it to her ear, rewinding with deft application of her fingers to the buttons, without looking. We hear some of their recent conversation quite distinctly—*

RECORDER: ". . . the cleaning lady . . . because you are insane . . ."

MRS. MAY *gets the playback set where she wants it. Reaches with the little machine across the desk, right into* MARIGOLD's *face.*
  A long, long pause.
  She lowers the tape machine slowly to the desk. Sits back very slowly.

MRS. MAY: All right—

MARIGOLD *slaps the recorder aside. Grabs one of the copies of her confession and tears it into confetti, dancing around and showering herself with it.*
  She stops.

MARIGOLD: "Homosexual maniac."

She grabs the second copy, shredding it and strewing the shreds, repeating the phrase a dozen different ways:

> Homosexual maniac. Homosexual maniac. Homosexual
> maniac. Homosexual maniac. Homosexual maniac. Homo-
> sexual maniac. Homosexual maniac. Homosexual maniac.
> Homosexual maniac. Homosexual maniac. Homosexual
> maniac. Homosexual maniac.

Meanwhile, she tears the third unsigned copy in half. Balls up one half, tosses it over her shoulder. Balls up the second half, tosses it.
Picks up the recorder. Holds it out, thumbs the Play button:

RECORDER: "Homosexual maniac."

She drops the recorder in the trash.
Pause.
MRS. MAY *gets up, turns slowly, shuts the blinds. Leaves the desk. Picks up the stack of magazines. Dignified, not cowed. Looks at* MARIGOLD. *Takes hold of the doorknob and turns to leave, but* MARIGOLD *stops her with a word—*

MARIGOLD: Cass . . . went down the Colorado River once. I saw him one spring, he stopped at my place in Dallas and said he was heading to Arizona. Gonna drive a raft for one of those outfits that takes you down the river and through the canyon. I asked him, "Cass—how'd they pick *you?*" "Oh, I met the owner of the company in this bar and I told him, Hey, I wouldn't mind a job like that. He asks do I have any rafting experience and I said, Hell yes, all over the rivers of South Texas, every damn river!" That's Cass! I don't think he'd ever been in a rowboat at this point. I don't think he'd splashed around in anything bigger than a stock pond. After he got out there, I tried to phone him one time; but the office up there in Grand Canyon country said, Yeah, he works for us, but he's out on a trip right now down the Colorado. What was that man's name?

MRS. MAY: Uh . . .

MARIGOLD: The explorer.

MRS. MAY: Uh. Powell. John, uh . . .

Pause.

MARIGOLD: Well . . . Cass came back through Dallas in the fall. He told me he drove a raft with eight passengers, three workers, and all their gear in it. Food, camping equipment, all of that. The second day they were floating along and he heard a strange sound growing and growing down the way. "Hey, Cookie, is that a train I hear downriver there?" he asked the cook. "What do you mean?" says the cook. "I mean it kind of rumbles and rumbles, do you hear that great big sound? Do they have a train track down this deep in a canyon?" "Wait a minute," the cook says. "Do you really don't know what that sound is? How many times have you run this river?" Cass says, "Hell, I never drove one of these things before in my life. I'm just picking it up as I go." "Get this raft over to the side," the cook says. And they spend the night by the river, and the cook tells him everything he can think of about shooting the rapids in a giant raft with a dozen people on board. "Next day we got up and put her in and started along. The rumble got bigger and bigger. Inside of thirty minutes it was just nonstop thunder filling the whole Grand Canyon, till we come around a curve, and the whole river looks like one big white monster avalanche of snow down over a field of boulders. I steered her into that mess and inside of five minutes I wrecked that thing so bad I don't believe they'll ever find the little rubber bits of it, if there's any left," he says. "But—the people loved it! Didn't nobody get hurt very bad, and we stopped the next raft that came by in a few hours and radioed for a helicopter and we all got choppered out. It was the best raft trip those people ever had!" The company didn't let him near the tiller again, you can bet. He spent the rest of the summer working as a helper.

Pause. MRS. MAY *shrugs.*

MARIGOLD: Isn't there a Lake Powell in Colorado or someplace like that?

MRS. MAY: Yes. In Colorado.

Pause.
     MRS. MAY *turns and leaves, shutting the door behind her. As it closes, the two of them stare at one another through the narrowing gap—*

BLACKOUT

We hear the door close in the dark.

2. Head Rolling and Rolling

A hotel coffee shop. A man in a suit, mid-forties, alone at a table. A woman walks in, business suit, mid-thirties. Looks around. Lights up when she sees the man.

WOMAN: Are you— (*Pause.*) You look just like—Bill Jenks?

MAN: Wild Bill—"The World's Only Snake with Legs." The Siberian Shaman.

WOMAN: Bill!

She joins him at the table. Pause.

Do you recognize me at all?

MAN: I don't think so.

WOMAN (*to invisible waiter*): Can I have a coffee? (*To* MAN:) I want to get really nervous. I brewed up six courtesy packs upstairs, that's all they had. I need to be creative . . . I don't know why I just plunked down. Is it okay? I never really knew you over in—just by reputation. I didn't think you had a sense of humor. I mean, "The world's only snake with legs." I didn't think you'd actually heard—It's well *meant*—res*pect*fully—

MAN: Fearfully—

WOMAN: Okay! Call a spade a spade. Although, the "Siberian Shaman"—is that new?

MAN: Sure. *I'm* new.

WOMAN: Really! But that's . . . you *are* different. There's an air almost about you . . .

MAN: The man who survived Siberia. Meaning District Nine.

WOMAN: Tell me about it!

MAN: I don't think I have to.

WOMAN: I just didn't think things like that ever got back to people.

MAN: Behind-the-back things.

WOMAN: Long as we're promoting candor!

MAN: Like how did old Wild Bill get wind of—

WOMAN: Yeah—have you got a snitch?

MAN: He didn't.

WOMAN: What.

MAN: I don't think he's heard it. But I have. Because I'm not him.

WOMAN: Who.

MAN: Bill Jenks.

WOMAN: . . . You're not Bill Jenks.

MAN: But wait a minute—wait a minute. I do *know* Bill Jenks—I spent forty-five minutes with him yesterday in his office. The Legless Snake himself. And I do agree I look like him.

WOMAN: Huh. Well.

Pause.

MAN: I'm down from Washington.

WOMAN: Sure . . . Are you District? Regional?

MAN: I'm Washington. I'm National.

WOMAN: Wow. You're not an Undersecretary or something.

MAN: No. I just report to a few. Chalmers . . . and Don Astasio . . . and Tina Ray.

WOMAN: Coffee! A warm-up . . .

MAN: And I'm kind of embarrassed to say I think I know your—

WOMAN (*overlapping*): How did you—*don't* be embarrassed—

MAN: —so I know about your situation.

Pause.

WOMAN: Oh.

MAN: Hey. So now it's *your* turn not to be embarrassed.

Pause.

WOMAN: Well, if you know, you know.

MAN: That's the spirit!

WOMAN: Really? What *is* the spirit? I mean, that's—I don't even know. Do you know the story of *Madame Butterfly*? The opera?

MAN: I'm not sure it's an opera, exactly.

WOMAN: Does it have something to do with a man—who has an affair—with a man dressed up as a woman? I mean, for twenty-five *years* or something?

MAN: Wow. No. I mean sure, possibly, it might, for all I know. I don't know.

WOMAN: Sure. Well— (*Pause.*) The Siberian Shaman. That's a new one. Why do they call him—

MAN: Jenks? Jenks got religion.

WOMAN: I think he was always *some*thing.

MAN: You mean like—

WOMAN: —something religious. Like he took it seriously.

MAN: After the transfer, he took it to another level. To a point well beyond seriously. Now for the last couple years he's been shepherd to his own little flock.

WOMAN: Really! You mean a pastor, a minister? Or . . .

MAN: Yeah, a shaman. He's applied for tax-exempt status.

WOMAN: Everybody you look at has some terrible secret, don't they?

MAN: He came to work this morning in a white minivan with lettering on the door that says "Worldwide Fellowship— Children of Jehovah." . . . You seem nervous.

WOMAN: I'd say I'm more a combination of stimulated and anxious.

MAN: Well, that would add up to . . . nervous.

WOMAN (*overlapping*): Nervous. But it's more as if I'm primed for this thing, I'm pumped, I'm ready, and at the same time I'm worried—

MAN: You'll do fine.

WOMAN: —more and more every minute.

MAN: It's one session and you're done. What's to worry about? Riggs? . . . You're not worried about *Riggs*—

WOMAN: Riggs who?

MAN: Riggs the wimp. You don't have to worry about Riggs. Just—that's who you're up against. There's Riggs, and Northup. And Toast.

WOMAN: Toast.

MAN: Jack Toast. It's an unusual name but it's not unheard of.

WOMAN: Who's Jack Toast?

MAN: Toast? . . . I'm—me. That's—

WOMAN: Toast.

TOAST: I thought you knew the lineup.

Pause.

WOMAN: Are you sure you have the right—

TOAST: I'm not sure. I just guessed. Are you Katherine Wendell?

WOMAN: Kate.

TOAST: John Toast.

They shake hands.

KATE: Well. (*Pause.*) Well. If I've met one-third of the team, I guess I should feel about thirty-three percent less nervous. (*She fumbles her cup but manages not to spill.*)

TOAST: I'm not a worry. I'd be a tiger in any investigation, but this isn't my investigation. I'm only monitoring.

KATE: Investigation?

TOAST: Interview.

KATE: Well, which is it? I was told—

TOAST: Interview. It's an interview.

KATE: Well, why did you say—

TOAST: Generally I do conduct investigations. But in this case that is not the case.

KATE: Well—

TOAST: I'm monitoring an interview.

KATE: Well, John—

TOAST: Jack.

KATE: —Jack, John—what's the difference?

TOAST: I prefer Jack.

KATE: Mr. *Toast* . . . What is the difference . . . between an interview and an investigation.

Pause.

TOAST (*after some thought*): An "investigation" might consist of a series of interviews. But an *interview* would be unique. Unrepeatable. An "investigation" would seek facts to be submitted in a report. An *interview* would seek an interchange to be reported in a memo. An "investigation" is terrifying. An *interview*—

KATE: *Isn't?* Then why am I terrified?

TOAST: You've got the jitters. Six pots of coffee—

KATE: *Why* are you *mon*itoring—

TOAST: Well, that's what I do.

KATE: I thought you conducted—

TOAST: I do. I *am* an investigator. In this case the monitoring process is part of a larger inquiry.

KATE: An inquiry? Now *that's* terrifying.

TOAST: Yes. (*Pause.*) It's the most terrifying thing in our business. But not for you.

KATE: No?

TOAST: Not in this case, because the inquiry isn't about you. It only has to do with your District . . . Look. Whenever your District has initiated a process to result in termination, inevitably that process—

KATE: Am I being *terminated*?

TOAST (*amused*): Uh. Wait a minute. Let's back up!

KATE: —Because I thought I was just gonna go in there, it takes about thirty minutes, describe the circumstances, her actions, Marigold Cassandra—I brought my notes—

TOAST: Hey— (*Mollifying gestures.*)

KATE: I didn't bring any notes about *me*.

TOAST: I can see how you might—

KATE: I really came to see the opera! This was just—

TOAST: Wait a second. All the way back—

KATE: *Madame Butterfly!* And now I'm being—

TOAST: Kate—

KATE: Oh! . . . You're firing *her*. *They*, I mean, the District. Not you.

TOAST: Let's back up. (*Pause.*) You came in. You looked around. I looked like whatsis—

KATE: The Siberian Shaman.

TOAST: —Jenks. Bill.

KATE: I *do* have the jitters. I'm sorry.

TOAST: We said hi: "Hi!" "Hi!" And here we are on the espresso express in a room full of Germans.

KATE: Germans. Oh—

TOAST: Yeah. I think so.

KATE: Well, it's *decorated*—

TOAST: Yeah. I thought it was just a gag. But listen—I thought it was a gimmick, I mean—they're speaking German.

Pause.

KATE: Do you think they can understand us? *I'm* sorry—

TOAST: Sure they can.

KATE: —nobody speaks *only* German . . . This is a hotel for Germans?

TOAST: Like they have in Germany, or someplace—

KATE: That's really—!

TOAST: —like wherever you go they have hotels for Americans. In Germany, for instance.

KATE: Is this going on all over America?

TOAST: Probably. I know they have the Meridien in Los Angeles. Or Orange County.

KATE: Another hotel full of Germans?

TOAST: Actually, they're French. The Meridien—

KATE: I'd love to stay in a Japanese hotel! But I mean—in America.

TOAST: Why not?

KATE: Or Japan. I guess Japan would make more sense.

TOAST: Why?

KATE: Well. Jack. Because it's—I don't know.

TOAST: Sure, okay—

KATE: Because it's a wish. If you're gonna wish for a Japanese hotel, you might as well wish for a Japanese hotel in Japan. Don't you think?

TOAST: Well, that doesn't seem like much of a wish. Japan would be full of Japanese hotels. You'd expect it. You wouldn't have to wish for it.

Pause.

KATE: So, your first name would be John?

TOAST: Yeah. Unless it was my middle name.

KATE: So which is it?

TOAST: Terrence. My first name—

KATE: Terrence John Toast?

TOAST: That is my entire name.

KATE: Darn.

TOAST: What.

KATE: My pen's stopped. (*Starts shaking a pen down.*) I'm taking notes sideways.

Pause.

TOAST: Notes?

KATE: Just— (*Pause.*) I'm just jaggin' on the java so—something to do with my hands. I'm not— (TOAST *silences her with a gesture.*)

TOAST: I don't think anyone should know about this, our—I guess this encounter. Coincidental encounter.

KATE: Oh. But so—am I supposed to walk into the conference, the interview, in—fifty-seven minutes and say hello and pretend— Can I expect you actually to be in the room?

TOAST: Why don't we just call it a conference.

KATE: Are you there? Monitoring? Or are you hiding some-place monitoring?

TOAST: I'm the first one in the room. I go in fifteen minutes early. I'm there when you all come in. You three come in together.

KATE: God. You look *just like* Bill Jenks.

TOAST: Bill Jenks brings you in. (*Pause.*) So we're all intro-duced. You and I. And them. Even though we're ac-quainted.

KATE: You and I.

TOAST: And them—Riggs and Northup. I know them.

KATE: But you pretend not to.

TOAST: No. I know them.

KATE: But you don't know me?

TOAST: I *flew with them* from Washington.

KATE: First class?

TOAST: Dream on.

KATE: I was just wondering who I was up against.

TOAST: Nobody. Not *against*. —Hey, you only see the first class types for the brief second before you're incinerated! *I'm* just—

KATE: So you're not the Incinerator. You're not the Terminator. You're not the Investigator. You're . . . Toast!

TOAST: I'm the Monitor. I don't say a word.

KATE: Let me just make a note of that.

TOAST: Can we back up? All the way up?

KATE: We keep backing *up,* Jack.

TOAST: I was sitting here—

KATE: —monitoring a room full of Germans—

TOAST: —minding my own goddamn business.

Pause.

By a complete coincidence—can we agree on that? By a complete coincidence. A random happenstance—

KATE: —two souls collided in Bavaria.

Pause.

TOAST: You know . . . I sort of feel like that. Not about meeting you, but, yes. About meeting you, and about your District, and a lot of other people have observed that District

Nine is a kind of *swamp,* or *Bavaria,* if you prefer, full of incompetents—

KATE: —full of snakes without legs—

TOAST: —that's right, where every simple personnel procedure becomes polluted. You're all too incompetent to weed out the incompetents! Inevitably, on appeal, the action gets *reversed,* they're reinstated with back pay and come back unmotivated, pissed off, and still incapable. And yes. The Legless Snake. A case in point.

KATE: Is it *with* legs? Or without? The snake.

TOAST: Whatever you do to the guy's legs, Jenks is the last idiot who'll ever transfer out of the Ninth. No more refugees. The bridges are blown. Bavaria is festering in its own pus. Therefore, Riggs and Northup, before conducting a simple Closure Interview—

KATE: Closure?

TOAST: Closure! Closure! An interview to put an end to the entire incident. Or at least to seal this particular compartment.

KATE: All right. Closure. So Riggs—

TOAST: So Riggs, and so Northup, they get flown out and briefed on Compartmentalization. And then *quizzed* on Compartmentalization. (*Pause.*) Compartmentalization. It's new. It's new because of your District. From now on, every investigation—

KATE: Investigation?

TOAST (*overlapping*): —will be approached as if the matter under scrutiny were divided into a number of separate compartments.

KATE: You said it *wasn't* an investigation—

TOAST: In your particular com*part*ment we are only conducting an "interview" . . . Look, it's really kind of an elegant concept. Would you like to hear it? (*Pause.*) The process of pollution is arrested by viewing the entire procedure as consisting of discrete units, or entities—compartments. Where proper procedure gets violated by idiots, or where for some reason pollution is threatening to render, for instance, a personnel action reversible, we seal that compartment off. By conducting a closure interview, in this case.

KATE: In this case.

TOAST: *Or:* in other cases. For instance. We go for bifurcation. We split the process into two separate processes. In the action to shitcan Marigold Cassandra it's this compartment—the issue between you and Marigold Cassandra . . . That's where the pollution is.

Pause.

KATE: So. Jack. (*Pause.*) How serious is this?

TOAST: You know better than to ask that.

KATE: Why? You've been reassuring me it *wasn't*—

TOAST: You know better than to ask that while you're taking notes.

KATE (*putting down pen*): Okay! There! I'm not! Okay?

Pause.

TOAST: Katherine . . . Can I ask you do destroy those notes?

KATE: Yes.

Pause.

TOAST: I'm not sure what was just agreed to.

KATE: You asked if you could ask. And I said yes.

TOAST: Yes: I can ask.

KATE: Yes. But. First. Just wait. Wait—*first* just tell me what's going on. *Then* ask me to trash the notes. And I think we'll have a deal.

Pause.

TOAST: Well, that's no deal at all, but I don't mind filling you in, because it's just what you're gonna find out ten minutes into the interview. In fact, it's exactly what you already know. Nothing more. All right. Now—can I back up a bit?

KATE: All the way to Genesis!

TOAST: June of three years ago. District Nine enters . . .

KATE: Wait. Start five years ago.

Pause.

TOAST (*after some thought*): Five years ago District Nine completes a lengthy investigation of Kernwood Farms which fails to yield satisfactory results. Leaving everybody bitter that "regulations have been flouted with impunity," and yes, I'm quoting from the report, which basically swore an oath of revenge. An oath never to give up on Kernwood Farms, which we all understood to be a blood oath to destroy, to trash, to strangle the Kernwood Farms Corporation and bury it and piss on its grave . . . But first an internal bloodbath commenced. Which amounted to nothing in the end. A few transfers.

KATE: Bill Jenks.

TOAST: Wild Bill. You bet. (*Pause.*) So that was Kernwood Investigation Number One.

KATE: Okay. Now three years ago.

TOAST: June. Thirty-six months ago. District Nine undertakes the second investigation of the Kernwood Farms Corporation. Within six months it's clear all the way to Washington that District— What District Nine has created is its own ridiculous Vietnam.

KATE: Bavaria invades the Far East.

TOAST: By forming independent units—

KATE: —*teams,* as Washington instructed—

TOAST: —and attempting coordination with the Food and Drug Administration—

KATE: —as Washington encouraged us to do—

TOAST: —such a massive fiasco of duplication and repetition and just plain running around ensued, that—now it's July, twenty-three months ago, the investigation in progress over a year—such a *fiasco* that a three-page overview submitted by some Kernwood attorney's *law clerk* to a *staffer* on the Hill results in Senate hearings. Televised.

KATE: Hey! On cable. C-Span. Big deal.

TOAST: Big deal, yeah. But the Senators listened raptly to descriptions of how Team One would show up waving a manifest for certain samples *just* loaded into vans by Team Three, while FDA teams got two, three, *four* separate search warrants going after the *same* items, convinced they were *hidden.* And then the hearings were *pre-empted* all of a sudden one day by a *miracle*—

KATE: I was on the ground—

TOAST: —the televised spectacle of seventeen—and I'm not talking about C-Span—

KATE: —tell me about it—

TOAST: —tell *me* about it, my boss delivered the apology for the Ag side—the spectacle of seven*teen* workers—the whole three-to-eleven shift—held, trapped, by armed agents in a *canning* factory. By armed agents of the Department of Agriculture? We don't *have* arms! We don't have agents! We're people!

KATE: I was at the farm. At the cannery. At the hearings.

TOAST: Seventeen workers—and a video camcorder. (*Pause.*) Weeping teenage gals in white hair nets and blue smocks eating jam with their little fingers. The tiny little black girl! That pretty little—

KATE: Tanya Cruz. She's an actress now. A sitcom. I don't think . . . She plays the daughter. It's not on the air yet. I don't think she sings.

Pause.

TOAST: And what was the worst?

Pause.

KATE: That everything looked so sanitary. (*Pause.*) You could not expect a germ to live anywhere near that lovely purity and innocence.

Pause.

TOAST: After that mess, the hearings resume, the testimony of what went on, and on, and on, and on, at Kernwood Farms: in the offices, the cannery, the transport division, in the *rows* of *grapes*, in the *dirt*. Agents repeating themselves like the Inquisition, different agents using the same words, the same phrases—

KATE: The same names—

TOAST: Taggart comes! Taggart goes! Then Taggart arrives followed later on that day by—Taggart! Three Taggarts? *Taggart* is not a common name.

KATE: Two Joneses.

TOAST: Jones is common.

KATE: Michaels—

TOAST: Chop off their heads!

KATE: I did! I tried! I'm trying—

TOAST: You were in charge of one head.

KATE: I put Miss Marigold's head on the block.

TOAST: And up steps Mrs. May for the kooty-grah. (*Pause.*) Boom! The phone rings . . . Oh yes. She got the news in the middle of Interrogation Number One.

KATE: Wow. An interrogation.

TOAST: Oh yeah . . . That's the procedure. A series of interrogations followed by a series of termination interviews. The Platform Interview. The Notification Interview. Transition Interview. And the whole time, the worker's head is rolling and rolling and rolling. All this is completely aside from any appeal process, of course.

KATE: Are you kidding me?

TOAST: Absurd, isn't it. All this time the head is rolling. Since the first written notification, which arrives by Federal Express. Which is not in the least bit Federal . . . We oughta be ashamed of that . . . But I guess we aren't . . . I know I'm not. (*Pause.*) Well, that's all that ever brings it to a stop, the Out-ductee just can't endlessly endure that horrible sensation of his head rolling and rolling. A series of pointless interviews . . .

KATE: The Out-ductee?

Pause.

TOAST: Once you understand we're all about absurdity . . . about pushing the limits of the absurd . . . you just have to try and outdo yourself.

Pause. They stare at each other electrically.

But when I said "back up," I didn't mean quite all the way into the last century. I meant . . . just to where you came in here and sat down with me.

KATE: At your invitation.

TOAST: Perhaps. Fine. You come in, you're looking a bit *lost* . . . There you are. So I—

KATE: So why?

TOAST: I didn't think we were connected. (*Shrugs.*) And I wanted to be.

KATE: So you're harassing me. Sexually.

TOAST: I thought you were a babe.

KATE: Jesus! You—

TOAST: Thought! Thought! I now appreciate that you are not in that category. You're a co-worker, your gender is invisible to me. But you asked why I— (*Gestures between them.*) And you received an answer.

KATE: Did you read his letter?

Pause.

TOAST: The one from the brother, this is.

KATE: Yes.

TOAST: Nope.

KATE: You didn't read it? Then how—

TOAST: Kate. *We don't take the letter seriously* . . . "Homosexual maniac"?

KATE: I thought you didn't—

TOAST: I didn't *read* it. But I sure had it quoted to me enough times. At least the homosexual maniac part. I rode with them on the plane, Riggs—

KATE: Riggs and Northup. Who I'm up against.

TOAST: No. We seal this letter business off. *Closure.* It can't contaminate, it can't feed, it will *die*.

KATE: So this is basically damage control.

Pause.

TOAST: Damage control is no longer a term with any real utility. As nomenclature it was too . . . apt. Compartmentalization is so much more elaborate and just so much more ridiculous. You discuss compartmentalization for ten minutes, you feel like all day you've been inhaling fumes. Everyone sounds like Munchkins . . . Throbbing Technicolor absurdity. (*Pause.*) Do you see what's happening? (KATE *shrugs helplessly.*) To sit across this table from somebody and speak the truth about our fate?

Pause.

KATE: Nobody in the whole department has ever talked like this to me before.

TOAST: And I've never talked like this to anyone. And only one person ever talked like this to me. And I'm sure *I* was the only one he ever— (*Pause.*) Manfred Dillman.

KATE: Man-fred Dill-man! . . . "A man first and last."

TOAST: Man-fred Dill-man. He was a man coming and going. He was the one. He sat me down in his office on his last day. I'd never spoken to him before. You know what people said about him? How long have you been with the Department?

KATE: Twelve years, almost. I knew of him.

TOAST: They used to call him the greatest bureaucrat next to J. Edgar Hoover. But they were wrong. He was greater.

KATE: Tell me.

TOAST: J. Edgar Hoover was a maestro. A campaigner. He parted his name on the side, for Christ's sake. A conniver. Dillman was a genius. Dillman was a poet . . . (*Intense, rapid:*) I'm sure he picked me entirely at random. He spoke to me for five minutes. He was wearing a brown suit. A yellow shirt. A blue string necktie fastened with a tarnished silver longhorn steer's . . . head. He invited me to push the limits of the absurd. To make that my vocation. He said, "We—are—surrealists." And he dismissed me. Now. Now don't you understand what's happening?

KATE: Well. All right—no.

TOAST: I'm giving you the formula for success, Kate. In exchange for those notes. I'm acting unilaterally. I'm utterly at your mercy.

Pause.
She hands them over. He holds her hand. Pause. Suddenly they're kissing. As they kiss:

KATE: What are we—doing—

TOAST: We're celebrating, honey—

KATE: Okay! Celebrating what?

TOAST: A supremely intimate moment. It's unrepeatable. (*Pause, kissing.*) They said you met him.

KATE: Who? . . . Yeah! Her brother walked up to me in a restaurant and sat down and called me a homosexual maniac!

TOAST: You didn't tell Georgina Jameson. I mean about the threats.

Pause. They separate as before.

KATE: Then he phoned me twice.

TOAST: You mean the brother—

KATE: —the brother. Get off his sister's back or he's gonna "blow the whistle." I thought he was crazy. He *is* crazy. I didn't think he'd—her brother—what if he did nothing? I'm spooked into denying accusations in advance. Then the accusations don't come. I flipped a coin. Tails. I waited him out.

TOAST: Damned if you do.

KATE: Damn right you're damned. We're all damned. *I—tossed—a coin.* (*Pause.*) What's gonna happen to me?

TOAST: Nothing. It's ludicrous. Just this interview. We'll close this off and get little old Marigold's termination back on track—

KATE: But *me.* What's gonna happen to *me?*

TOAST: I don't think . . .

Pause.

KATE: We are. We're all damned. Aren't we. Don't tell me you don't think. Tell me yes or no. Are we damned?

TOAST: Yes.

KATE: We're damned.

TOAST: Yes.

KATE: Are you upstairs?

TOAST: . . . Yes.

KATE (*peering at her watch*): How long—

TOAST (*also peering at her watch*): Forty, forty-five—figure five minutes to walk over there—

KATE: I want you to take me upstairs. And then I want you to take me. Take me any way you want. And then I want you to drag me into that conference room. And then I want you to do whatever you want to me. Whatever you want.

Pause. They kiss again, softly and beautifully, one long loving kiss.

BLACKOUT

3. Hellhound on My Trail

Lights come up dimly on a room at the Paradise or Starlight or Aces Motel. The TV plays soundlessly, broadcasting a changing light. On the bed MARK CASSANDRA, *known as* CASS, *sleeps in his jeans. The curtains are drawn.*

In the upstage wall, the bathroom door stands open, and the bathroom is full of daylight. A toilet, and a small window above it. Just outside the bathroom is the sink. Right of bed, a chest of drawers. Couple of lamps, etc. At stage left, a green door and a curtained window.

CASS *wakes abruptly. Swings around and sits up as if he knows exactly what he should be doing right now, then realizes he doesn't. Begins coughing—a smoker. Looks around, completely disoriented. Peers at the TV. He's sitting on the remote—digs it out and points:*

WOMAN'S TV VOICE: —leaves twenty-two days, Jim, just twenty-two days in which to seize this *golden* opportunity, twenty-two days. And *that's*—

CASS *hits the mute, lies back down, frisks himself for a smoke, reaches out a hand to the nightstand, clearing his throat. His hand finds a revolver. He sits up. His throat-clearing turns to screaming moans. He leaps out of bed and cuts on the lamp.*

He examines the gun fearfully: sniffs at the gun barrel, opens out the cylinder and spins it, tosses the thing down and starts to dress.

CASS: *Oh yeah, oh yeah, oh yeah . . .*

(*Muttering, rapid, searching around:*) Oh yeah, oh yeah, we got the shit-hole motel, we got the puke on the sheets, we got the gun with a bullet missing . . . We're gonna bust in with a warrant and ride you to the principal's office in the electric chair. You got a toothbrush? Do you at least have that? You got one boot. How about a sock then? (*Finds his smokes on the floor, sticks one in his mouth.*) LIGHTER? LIGHTER? . . . Will you at least get rid of the evidence? Will you at least do that?

He strips a pillow, wipes the gun, wraps it in the pillowcase, and, shoving open the bathroom window, starts to drop it outside.

He turns, pauses, standing in the bathroom as in a box of light, and then sticks his hand into the pillowcase, lets it drop—the gun's in his hand.

He puts the barrel in his mouth, first removing his unlit cigarette. Pause. He puts the smoke in his mouth and tries putting the gun in his ear. Pause. He closes his eyes. Pause. He reaches in his pants pocket, takes out a lighter, fires up his Kool. Opens his eyes. Lowers the gun from his head.

He jams the pistol in the pillowcase, drops it out the window with a shudder.

Coming back toward the bed, he finds his Hawaiian-style shirt draped on a chair. He dons the shirt, finding two bullet holes in the area of the waistline. He lines them up—an entrance and an exit— threading his finger through both and wiggling it, astonished.

Checking his own abdomen, he finds a burn mark in the corresponding area along his ribs.

Heads over to the room's window, opens the curtains. Freezes, looking at some objects on the sill. Picks one up—a small plastic-wrapped packet. Tears a hole in it, tastes some of the contents on the tip of his tongue.

He whips back and forth a couple times, then grabs half a dozen of the packets (there are nine in a row on the sill, if we could make them out) and rushes to the john and starts tearing them open and flushing them.

But the toilet clogs. He hunts deliriously—

CASS: Plunger! PLUNGER!

—nothing. He starts jamming the packets down the toilet with his hand—we're mostly looking at his rear end throughout this operation and listening to his frenzied moans and incoherent exclamations.

He rushes back to the bedroom window, picks up the last three packets in both his hands. He holds them against his chest.

MAN'S VOICE: Hey.

A hand bangs on the screen and CASS *spasms, the three packets go flying. He tries to gather them together surreptitiously with a toe while talking to the man outside his window:*

MAN: Checkout is twelve noon, dude.

CASS: Fine.

MAN: You got that?

CASS: I'm on it! It's a lock! That's what "fine" means!

MAN: Do you know what time it is now?

CASS: I do know, yeah. What about it?

MAN: Then tell me.

CASS: No.

MAN: It's eleven-forty. Do you even know what day it is?

CASS: It's today all day. What about it?

MAN: If you know, then why don't you tell me?

CASS: Because I don't go walking up to people who I don't even know who they're supposed to be and start telling them completely obvious stuff, man.

MAN: Come on, impress me: What day is it?

CASS: Who are you?

MAN: Somebody you won't even give the time of day.

CASS: It's eleven-forty!

He shuts the window. Draws the curtains fast.

He's terribly shaken. Confused, terrified, without a clue.

He leaps to the phone and yanks up the receiver as if it were ringing, but it's not. He takes two breaths, hits some buttons. Intones his name slowly for a collect call:

CASS: Mark—Cassandra. (*Pause.*) Hey, is Bob Cornfield—is that you, Bob? It's Cass, buddy. Mark, Mark *Cassandra. Cass.* (*Pause.*) I know, but this ain't the time to be joking—if you know me *say* you know me, because I don't know if anybody knows me or even where I *am*. (*Pause.*) I don't *know* where I am. (*Pause.*) Look, Bob, listen to me. I was asleep. I woke up. There's a gun beside me with bullets missing. I think there's bullet holes in my shirt. Here's the situation. I don't know where I am. And there's nine ounces of I think it's *skag,* man, all lined up in a row real pretty on my windowsill where everybody can just walk idly by like it's the Museum of Heroin. (*Pause.*) I flushed it! I'm flushing it! Or I guess it's coke—my tongue is numb. (*He proceeds to finish the flushing operation while dragging the phone around and talking.*) Well, it's a pretty good room. It's not bad. At least there's a phone. (*Pauses to take two big snorts of the powder before flushing the last of it.*) I don't know! Probably the stuff was here when I got here! It must've been! (*Pause.*) What—hey—*what* maids? They open the door, they reach in and dip the ash off their cigarette and they're gone, *they* don't notice. I used to live with a chick who cleaned rooms, you remember Jeannie, Jeannie, Jeannie, Jeannie Bailey? (*He glances into the bath-room.*) Okay, the towels, yeah, they're fresh towels. (*Pause.*) Well, perhaps they didn't wish to disturb the drugs and weapons of the former occupant, Bob. (*Pause—pause—pause—he's cut off each time he takes a breath to speak.*) All right. (*He lets the phone dangle. Pause. Then:*) You still there, Bob? All right. This situation is the outcome of shit that has been done. And I admit whatever was done must've involved me. (*Pause.*) Last thing I remember I was in a casino in Tonopah. I was on the bus, it was like a rest stop so you can nip in real quick and lose your life savings and get a sandwich. I had one quarter left. I put it in a slot—bang, I hit for five bucks. My last quarter! Can you believe that! Life can— (*Pause.*) I went to the bar. I ordered a sandwich. I ordered a drink— hey, what *day* is it? (*Pause.*) Tequila. (*Pause.*) I DON'T *KNOW* WHERE I AM! I think maybe I've been taken away! Like if I look out the window there'll be nothing out there but outer space! (*Pause.*) No, I did, I looked out both sides, there's like a dirt field and an interstate, and the other side is a swimming pool and rooms with blue doors with *motherfucker!—cocksucker!—sonofabitch cunt fuck you whore!* and words like that scratched all over 'em . . .

He opens the curtains—the MAN *is still there—both start—he shuts the curtains fast.*

It's probably still Tonopah. But it might be Zimbabwe. I'm a long ways from Ukiah, especially if I'm hitching, that's for sure. I mean I'd have to hitch down Route Eighty, I figure, over to Route Five, and go—I'd have to *find* Route Eighty. I'd have to find out where *here* is. Where I *am.* So therefore—*if* I had the price of a bus ride, and something to eat on— Hey! Yer my *sponsor!* (*Pause.*) Well, I *will* come see you, when I (*click!*)—get there . . . (*He thumbs the button down, holds the receiver, looks at it:*) Look . . . I have done something. I did something . . . (*Pause. Hangs up, holding phone in his lap.*) "Whenever anyone, anywhere, reaches out for help, I want the hand of Alcoholics Anonymous to always be there. And for that, I am responsible."

Holding the phone in one hand, he yanks the curtains open again. The guy's still there.

CASS: Hey, if you—do you need to talk to me?

MAN: Well—

CASS: Because do you see this? This is a phone. Ever see one? You can call me.

MAN: Actually, you're on the phone.

CASS *yanks the curtains closed.*

Pause.
    Door goes Knock Knock.
    Pause. CASS *puts the phone down and opens the door halfway.*

MAN: Mr. Cassandra?

CASS: Who am I talking to, please?

MAN: I'm Agent Salazar with the Federal Bureau of Investigation.

CASS: I don't wanna talk to you.

The MAN *holds out an ID and badge.* CASS *peers at them.*

CASS: Salazar, that's a funny name for a blond guy. Practically an albino guy. We are not going to have a conversation.

SALAZAR: Well, we certainly don't have to. But we've been talking just a little here already, haven't we? Is it so horrible? . . . On a scale of one to ten?

CASS. Bee-low zero.

SALAZAR: You know why I was so nasty just a couple minutes ago? Have you heard of the good-cop bad-cop routine? I was being the bad cop. That was stupid.

CASS: It *was* stupid.

SALAZAR: I was just trying it out.

CASS: Yer too stupid to cough.

Pause.
   SALAZAR *coughs.*

SALAZAR: Sorry—I wasn't—

CASS (*overlapping*): I hate to be rude—

SALAZAR: No! You're not being rude. You're being a lot more pleasant than some folks. Last month—three weeks ago—in connection with my work—I got thrown out of a car. In connection with some undercover work. You can bet *that*—did I say it was moving? I got thrown out going about, nearly, thirty. I could do that ten more times in a row, and I'd be dead every time. I was born lucky. I really believe that. What about you?

CASS: I don't know.

SALAZAR: Would you say you've been generally pretty lucky? On a scale of one—

CASS: Extremely far down below zero. But! I put my last quarter in a slot there in I think Tonopah, I think, and . . .

Pause.

SALAZAR: Really hot out here.

CASS: You think it's cooler in here? Some fool left the window wide open all night.

SALAZAR: It'll break a hundred today. My prediction, a hundred and one by three P.M.

CASS: It's thermometer weather.

SALAZAR: What does that mean?

CASS: Thermometer weather? . . . Uh.

SALAZAR: I don't think I've heard that expression before.

CASS: Yeah. Shit. I'm doing it again . . . Have you ever been sitting at a bar and you hear a guy maybe polishing up like the tip of his cue stick, man, and you just know he's gonna lay it aside—he's laying it aside; he's getting out a knife; he's stepping over behind you and he's gonna ram that knife right through yer spine? Well, I do, I get that feeling, I do, a lot. And a lot of other people do, too. I can tell which ones just by the way they're sitting there . . . *Or:* You're sitting there with a cup of coffee, and a leaf blows into your cup. You fish it out and go on with another sip, but you didn't know it was a poison leaf. I mean, oleander grows all over the West, and it's poison enough to kill large animals. Oleander kills horses. And you take a sip of oleander coffee and blow your motor right there and keel over dead. (*Suddenly blithe:*) Come in! (*As* SALAZAR *obliges:*) Look, I freely admit I never should've gone to Vegas. I don't do big towns at all like a gentleman, not anymore. I get all stirred up, I get— It's all the *familiar faces*. Do you know what I'm talking about? Everybody looks like somebody you used to know, or at least there's some family resemblance. Running up to people with your arms out— whoops! Sorry, man, just took a false read on your face. Then when I'm completely certain—Jack Tilsdale! All these years! And he says, No, I'm not Jack Tilsdale. Quite the opposite. I *killed* Jack Tilsdale. I ran him *over*. He stepped funny in the traffic!

SALAZAR: You *have* a right to remain silent . . .

CASS: Hey there, I clearly realize a lot of people would censor themselves. I would too. But I got a planet rolling down on me, and I'm already squirming in the shadow, brother. We might only have a couple minutes for us to do our fate. Maybe a few hours, I don't know. But I do know it's absolutely no more than twenty-two days.

SALAZAR: Our fate? Mark. Hey.

CASS: I go by Cass.

SALAZAR: Cass. Cass. And where'd you get this twenty-two days?

CASS: Where? Have you ever seen a woman bone-naked when she was totally dressed? We all have these powers. But they're on, they're off. Very few of us ever get to control them. They come and go.

SALAZAR *goes to the sink, draws a glass of water, slakes his thirst. Pokes his head in the bathroom, shuts the door to it. Turns to* CASS.

SALAZAR: Your name is Mark Cassandra. You go by "Cass." You grew up in Texas—Odessa. Your mother is serving a long sentence for vehicular homicide. Your dad and your stepmom have recently been divorced. Your sister's on suspension from the U.S. Department of Agriculture. Your two brothers both have warrants out and both brothers are whereabouts unknown. You, yourself, live generally in Ukiah, California, but you get around impressively: You report you were recently in Las Vegas. You report you played a slot machine in Tonopah. We put you in Dallas on Thursday and Houston last Friday night.

CASS: Dallas? Houston? You mean to say Texas?

SALAZAR: I mean to say and I do say. Dallas. Houston. Texas.

CASS: I'm back in Texas?

SALAZAR: Back in Texas.

From a neighboring room a radio comes on, faintly playing something exotic, like "Maria Tudor" by Trio Bulgarka . . . CASS *bangs the wall—*

CASS: HEY. I got a headache!

—and the music stops.

SALAZAR: Back in Texas as of Thursday night.

SALAZAR *turns the TV volume up and then down quickly—*

TV: —killed in a fall from a roller coaster—

SALAZAR *straightens the curtains, eliminating gaps.* CASS *keeps still.*
SALAZAR *turns to him.*
  Music resumes softly.

SALAZAR: Back in Texas at the Lu Anne Motel: the Green
  Room. "Of all the rooms on earth . . ." This room! The
  Green Room! Can I tell you?

Pause. CASS *gestures: "Play on."*

SALAZAR: We were kids, you and I were—I was thirteen, I don't
  know about you—when they pulled off the biggest cash robbery in Texas history, right here not fifty miles from Houston.

CASS: We're fifty miles from Houston?

SALAZAR: Right up there on Highway Twenty-two. A Brinks
  armored truck with a driver and one guard, carrying close
  to twenty million dollars cash, turned north off the interstate and started up that long incline out of town . . . It's a
  gradual hill about fifteen miles long.

CASS *finds a cigarette butt.* SALAZAR *picks up the lighter and gives
him a light. Music's still playing.*

  That time of year the cotton fields were barren. Just huge
  fields of plain dirt with millions of empty furrows all lined
  up and marching away over the hills. It makes you sad.

Dead-looking oaks, flat gray grass. Ghost dogs. Dust devils. Butterflies and candy wrappers chasing along on the wind. The sad little road. It does make you sad. And this armor-plated truck crawling on the edge of Texas like a bug . . . And as it climbed up and up, the truck went slower and slower. "I *think* I can, I *think* I can . . ." Until near the top of the grade it wasn't doing any better than ten, fifteen miles an hour. At that point a General Motors pickup truck full of armed men from a right-wing paramilitary gang called "The Order" swung around from behind, and they held up a sign saying "PULL OVER OR DIE." (*Pause.* CASS puts out his cigarette.) They had some big guns. Mean ordnance. M-sixteens and stuff like that, shoot right through a bullet-proof window. The guards pulled over and gave up dozens of sacks of cash totaling just about twenty million dollars . . . It's not the money. The money doesn't count. Only the hugeness and strangeness of the number. Twenty million. Twenty million. It's like a *theory.* Twenty million. (*Pause.*) The robbers departed and split up into three groups. One bunch camped out on Orr Springs Road with ten million bucks. Another bunch went up to their headquarters in eastern Washington, also with several million dollars. And two men took the guns and a few hundred thousand to the Lu Anne Motel. This motel. Our motel. (SALAZAR *pauses while he lights another cigarette butt for* CASS.) The two guys stayed in this room after the robbery. (*Pause.*) When they got up the next day they looked out the window and what should they see parked out there but the same Brinks truck they knocked over yesterday. The FBI and the Marshals and the two Brinks guys were checked in here, too, they filled the whole place! Man, those two bad boys tiptoed out of town. They left their guns and the cash in an olive-green duffel bag under this bed, and nobody found it for eighteen months. (*Peering under the bed:*) It stained the rug green. See?

CASS (*also peering*): Kind of. Yeah . . .

Somewhere in here the music stops . . .

SALAZAR: They call this the Green Room. They really oughta charge extra for this room but they don't. (*Pause.*) Right here. We're right in the middle of the history of crime. That's the whole feeling I want you to share with me.

CASS: Thank you. (*Pause.*) That is a fantastically realistic ID you have there.

SALAZAR: Thanks. It was very expensive. It actually *is* real. All but the picture.

CASS: What happened to the real Agent Salazar?

SALAZAR: I'm asking the questions.

CASS: Yeah?

SALAZAR: Yeah.

CASS: But didn't I just ask you one? And didn't you answer me back with something that wasn't a question? In fact aren't I just asking a whole string of 'em one-two-three right now? . . . What happened to him.

SALAZAR: Take a guess.

CASS: He got thrown out of a moving car.

SALAZAR: I'm not here to kill you.

CASS: I know! You would never do that.

SALAZAR: What kind of a gun do I have? (CASS *shrugs.*) A sweet little nine.

CASS: But it's strictly for self-defense. (*As* SALAZAR *draws the gun and points it upward:*) You in the Agency adhere to that policy.

SALAZAR: But I'm not with the Agency.

CASS: But you *feel* like you are.

SALAZAR: Not really . . . No.

Pause.

CASS: What are you after?

SALAZAR: What am *I* after? The question is, what are *we* after?

CASS: Who is "we" supposed to be?

SALAZAR: I'll tell you who we *aren't.* "We" are not me and you. "We" are me and mainly some other people. Practically not myself at all. My role here is really that of an agent. Just—

not an agent of the FBI . . . An agent, a—I hate to call myself a "tool"—

CASS: An instrument.

SALAZAR: Right enough.

CASS: An instrument of the Law.

SALAZAR: You wish!

CASS: Here we go.

SALAZAR: The Law just locks you up and loses you. At the worst they squirt you full of poison and throw you in a grave. My people don't stop there.

CASS: I wouldn't think so.

SALAZAR: My people won't hesitate to wipe out your entire family in a fireball. If possible your whole town.

CASS: I know the type.

SALAZAR: They'll blow up the hospital you were born in. Slow-roast the guy who was the doctor at your birth.

CASS: I said I know the type.

SALAZAR: And that's just for spittin' on a rainy day.

CASS: WHAT DO THEY *WANT*?

Pause. SALAZAR *puts the gun in his belt.*

SALAZAR: We'd like to review the last couple of days with you, Mark. Cass.

CASS: Review away.

SALAZAR: Let's go over your activities of the last, let's say, forty-eight hours.

CASS: Can't help you there.

SALAZAR: Then maybe you're in need of a nine-millimeter attitude adjustment, pal.

CASS: You can adjust me to death, I can't help you—I'm drawing a blank since Tonopah! And you tell me it's Houston now?

SALAZAR: According to our information it's been Houston since at least Friday.

CASS: And today is—

SALAZAR: Tuesday.

CASS: And Tonopah was a Wednesday. The first tequila went down at noon. I been on a pretty mean run.

SALAZAR: Are you pleading amnesia?

CASS: That's gonna have to be my . . . yes.

SALAZAR: Have you heard of the Dead Sea Scrolls?

CASS: Haven't most people? . . . Sure . . . Not with my full attention.

SALAZAR: Well, you're just typical. Don't feel bad.

CASS: I don't. Who said I did?

SALAZAR: The Dead Sea Scrolls are an important revelation to mankind. They were found, dozens of papyrus scrolls, by three brothers in a cave. You know what papyrus is?

CASS: Sure. I forget. I used to.

SALAZAR: Paper, basically, of an antique process—

CASS: I know what cunnilingus is. It's basically cunt-licking. That's if you go ahead and speak American.

SALAZAR: All right. Will do . . . These three brothers in Egypt retired to a cave with the heart of a man they'd just murdered for revenge. He'd killed one of their family, and they'd taken his life in return. Now they intended to go into this dark place and eat their victim's heart. That's how they do things in Egypt. And they stumbled across the Scrolls, and the rest is history.

CASS: Did they eat the man's heart?

SALAZAR: It's not important.

CASS: Then you don't know the first thing about telling a story.

SALAZAR: Yes, they ate his heart! It was still warm, it went down like candy, blood dripping off their beards! They laughed and laughed because they hated him so much, but even eating his heart couldn't quench their hatred, and they died wishing they could kill him again! And then they brought out the ancient Scrolls that have taught us so much, so much—

Pause.

CASS: And so these people. Your people.

SALAZAR: You wanna know who.

CASS: I know already.

SALAZAR: What. Did you see the van?

CASS: Just tell me who.

SALAZAR: My people? The people who can get to you anywhere. Any time, any place. Here. Now. (*Pause.*) They can call you on that phone.

He points to the phone.

CASS: All right . . . Come on . . . Come on . . . We're waiting. They're busy. Blabbing in the ear of the President.

SALAZAR stays *focused on the boring spectacle of the telephone. But* CASS *looks away. Wanders around. Stands at the sink. Rubs his face. Looks at the faucet. Puts his hand out to the spigot. Just as he grips the handle, the phone rings. He jumps a mile. He stalls; lunges for it, reaches out; stalls dead. After the third ring, it quits.*
    Pause. The two men stare at one another until:

CASS: HA! HA! You think I don't know who you are? You think I wasn't waiting for you all along? (*Pause.*) When I stand on the plain up there in the middle of the state? And it's dark night and not a breath of wind? Oh, you're moving, moving, moving. You've got your nose in my tracks and your lust is like a knife just cutting through, and cutting through, and it'll cut through everything to find my heart. I been *waiting* for you . . . (*Shakes himself.*) Aah. It can't be. You're the Law. Government people gone rotten. Who are you? The DEA? The FDA? . . . The D of A.

SALAZAR: The D of A? No way. The C of J.

CASS: The C of J? The C of J?

SALAZAR: I thought you saw the van. With the logo.

CASS: I didn't see a van. If I did, I wouldn't take notes. The C of J?

SALAZAR: Yeah. The Children of Jehovah.

CASS: Like—"Jehovah." (*Pause.*) You . . . are a Jehovah's Witness.

SALAZAR: Absolutely—no no no! Far from it. Let me tell you about *those* folks. The Jehovah's Witnesses? (*While speaking he rummages around and finds the Gideon Bible and expertly locates a page.*) The JWs are false prophets, friend. Simply consider this verse—"How shall we know the word which the Lord hath not spoken? . . . When a prophet speaketh in the name of the Lord, if the thing follow not, nor come to pass, that is the thing which the Lord hath not spoken, but the prophet hath spoken it presumptuously: thou shalt not be afraid of him." Dooteronomy eighteen: twenty-one . . . *and* twenty-two.

CASS: You know what? That sounds like a nightmare hand of blackjack. Somebody hit twenty-one!

SALAZAR: The JWs predicted the End in 1914. The end of the world. The Second Coming of Jesus. 1914. Well. 1914 came and went. Where was Jesus?

CASS: Uh. I don't know.

SALAZAR: Exactly! Dooteronomy eighteen twenty-one twenty-two. Thou shalt not be afraid of the JWs.

CASS: Well. You've got them folks coming and going.

SALAZAR: We know 'em up and down, that's right.

CASS: That's right. And back and forth.

SALAZAR: That's right.

CASS: You might as well be one.

SALAZAR: Formerly I was.

CASS: You?

SALAZAR: I was. A lot of us. Yes. Formerly.

CASS: But you bailed.

SALAZAR: We all did. All the Children of Jehovah. Because the Witnesses are completely polluted. The Witnesses don't acknowledge the divinity of Christ. Did you know that? . . . Do you know what divinity is?

CASS: Like the scene with the animals and the manger. With the frankincense and myrrh—those people.

SALAZAR: Oh! thou generation of vipers!

CASS: I know what a viper is, it's a snake, and I'm proud to be one. And I know what *divinity* . . . Just don't go quizzing me on frankincense and myrrh . . .

SALAZAR: That's the *nativity*—the birth of Jesus. *Divinity* means he's God, he's divine. Jesus walked on the water. He quelled the stormy seas, he turned water into wine. He spit in a blind man's eyes and that man did see and shout. He rolled away the stone on his own grave and descended into

Hell and freed the captive spirits. And still the JWs don't believe he's God!

CASS: But you guys do.

SALAZAR: Well. No. We don't. But for completely different reasons.

CASS: *Oh* yeah.

SALAZAR: Yeah. *They* get it from the Book of Revelation. *We* get it from the Dead Sea Scrolls.

CASS: So a gang of them Jehovah Witnesses broke off—

SALAZAR: A large gang—a group, a very large group—

CASS: You broke away, you formed your own branch—

SALAZAR: We're not a *branch*. If *they're* a tree, then *we're* a tree. We've got our own roots, our own soil—

CASS: *Hey.* (*Pause.*) Wow. I'm not gonna dialogue religion with a —! People accuse *me* to be a speed-mouth little jazzbo . . .

SALAZAR: We're not in any way affiliated and our movement is self-sustaining, is all I'm . . . It comes from *God* . . .

CASS: So you left the outfit; you guys and gals, the Children of Jehovah; you fixed yourselves up in a church someplace and bought a vehicle and painted your name on the side and drove to my door, and here we are. And here is my question: I'd like you to state your purpose today.

SALAZAR: That I came to your door.

CASS: And made threats.

SALAZAR: Those were only for-instances.

CASS: Like wiping out my whole town, for instance.

SALAZAR: *You* were saying things too. We were riffing. We were joshing.

CASS: We were jiving. What do you people *want*?

SALAZAR: (*pointing the gun*): We want our effing *drugs* back, mate.

Pause.

CASS: Your *drugs*.

SALAZAR: That's right.

CASS: *Your* drugs!

SALAZAR: Yes *indeed*.

CASS: So you people in the Swords of Jesus or, you guys are—a coke-pushing religious cult.

SALAZAR: Not by intention.

CASS: *Accidently.*

SALAZAR: To keep talking with you would involve you being able to appreciate the complications of the human heart. But you, you're a kid, you're a pagan—

CASS: Hey now, I been to church—

SALAZAR: You've never been driven to your knees in the pit when you can't even raise your head to see how deep down you've fallen—

CASS: You should've had a little peek at me when I woke up not an hour ago.

SALAZAR: It's not a joke.

SALAZAR *wiggles the gun.* CASS *grapples it to his own breastbone and leans into it with his arms open wide.*

CASS: It's *not* a joke. Talk about the wrong side of the bed. I know how you can wake up on the wrong side of the universe. And you went to bed just hoping to be okay like everybody else is.

SALAZAR *is startled. He draws the gun back carefully from* CASS's *chest; puts it away.*

SALAZAR: And what's your crime? Did you steal? Did you lie? Is your whole life one big rip-off? Who did you kill? Did you kill somebody?

CASS: Not in so many words.

SALAZAR: Not in so many— Kill. How many words is kill? It's one word. (*Pause.*) Who did you kill, Cassandra?

Pause.

CASS: Don't call me Cassandra by itself. It's why I never went in the Army. I knew the sergeant would call me "Cassandra" every minute. Plus I won't take bossing, I can't take orders, I'm not built for it.

A long pause while SALAZAR *outwaits him.*

I lost a woman on this raft trip where we were on the Colorado River a couple years back. Or three years exactly.

SALAZAR (*sincerely*): That's too bad.

CASS: One of these days there's someone coming through that door. He won't look like the Devil. But it'll be him. (*Pause.* CASS *drifts with his thoughts until* SALAZAR *clears his throat.*) She fell, climbing around on the rocks where she shouldn't. That was her style. She was a cranky little—well, I ain't gonna call her a bitch: she's dead. But that's what she was. One of those pretty little people like to make everything a problem—like it's time to eat, I'm not hungry—it's time for coffee, I want tea—it's bedtime and we're all dog tired, I wanna have a *chat*—it's time to go, everybody's in the raft . . . (*Pause.*)

SALAZAR: Everybody's in the raft . . .

CASS: A very stylish type, every minute stylish. You seen 'em. But I bet you never talked to one. There's a lot of 'em—your usual tall Coppertone blonde in a white halter, white shorts, white spike heels, and she's a zigzaggy reflection across the hood of a big old red Cadillac, a red one—"Eldorado." Life looks like fun when you reflect it across a red Eldorado.

Pause.

SALAZAR: And?

CASS: And?

SALAZAR: And few of us drive Eldorados.

CASS: Right.

Pause.

SALAZAR: The woman.

CASS: Right.

SALAZAR: . . . Everybody's in the raft.

CASS: Yep. (*Pause.*) And as usual, where is she? She's off on a personal hike and somebody's got to track her down. One of those people. This wasn't a hiking trip. We were utilizing the waterways. So I got after her. Now. Here's one for you. She was half a mile up a trail, way up on a ledge all alone with her shorts down and her butt out over the air, peeing. It was spattering down on the rocks, going down like pebbles and making a clatter must have been eighty feet below. Then she started to switch her footing and just went over backward. I saw her go down, but I didn't see her land. She didn't give any indication. Not the smallest yip till when she hit, and then she said, Hu-uhhhh. Just the air going out through her voice. (*Pause.*) I had to radio back and get us choppered out. Later on I just told people we wrecked, like my sister, I told her . . . Which we did, but it wasn't that big a deal. We hauled out and dried off and put back in, it wasn't nothin'.

SALAZAR: These things happen, in a fallen world.

CASS: My sister is all right. There's a lot of twisted people on the surface of the earth, plenty of fakes, and snakes, and harlot queens and one-eyed jacks. Almost all of us, let's face it. But not her. Not my sister. She's fine. Her name is Marigold.

SALAZAR: I'm sure Marigold is fine.

Pause.

CASS: Here's one for you, chief. The thing of it is I think that woman that time—I think she saw me watching her. I think the surprise of it made her fall.

SALAZAR: Our hearts and souls are sought continually by the Devil.

CASS: That ain't news.

SALAZAR: We could help you. Join us!

CASS: Bite me! (*Staring hard at the phone:*) It's between me and my fate.

Pause. CASS *staring at the phone—*

SALAZAR: What are you up to?

CASS: I'm praying for that phone to ring.

SALAZAR'*s gaze is drawn to the TV.*

SALAZAR: Hey— (*Looks back and forth between TV and phone.*) Turn this up—that phone ain't gonna ring. Turn it— (*He turns up the TV.*)

NEWS VOICE: —in an underground shopping mall in Engle-town, New Jersey, will convene a panel to sift through the results of the massive investigation. Survivors of the terrible blaze—

SALAZAR (*turning TV down*): God told Job some things that were just flat-out nasty. Like: Can you make a forest full of trees a hundred years old and then fill that forest with snow? Can you make an elephant, can you manufacture a whale? Who do you think whomped up this whole shebang? Can you at least admit something's going on here bigger than you, something majestic? "Hast thou walked in the search of the depth, hast thou entered the springs of the sea?" (*He turns TV up.*)

NEWS VOICE: —huge fireballs propelled through stores by eerie winds created by abrupt temperature changes in the four-level mile-and-a-half-square area beneath this sleepy suburb. Witnesses to the holocaust—

CASS (*turning TV down*): I believe in God.

SALAZAR: Then what's your problem?

CASS: I think he's mean. I think he's an asshole.

NEWS VOICE (*as* CASS *turns TV up*): —crushing themselves through plate glass windows, and shoppers carried by escalators into the flames. Eighty-seven dead have been recovered, and one stretch of hallway remains—

CASS (*stabbing the Off button*): Carried into the flames. (*Pause.*) I woke up this morning with somebody's pistol.

SALAZAR: In bed? It's fortunate for you you didn't shoot your weenie off.

CASS: I been on a pretty mean run the last better than a week. My memory's coming back in drips and drabs.

SALAZAR: I can't help you there.

CASS: You helped me. You scared me. You jolted my MIND. Salazar—you're quietly scary. You've got a crazy way about you . . . "You too could have a career in law enforcement."

SALAZAR: I come in peace. But I mean business.

CASS: Three people set this up—a woman named Kate Wendell, and a guy, I think it's her boyfriend, his name is Jack she called him. And a guy I never did get his name. Looks like his brother.

SALAZAR: Whose brother?

CASS: Jack's brother.

SALAZAR: He looks like Jack's brother. Bill Jenks.

CASS: You know the guy?

SALAZAR: Sure. Brother Jenks? He's kind of—he started the Children of Jehovah.

CASS: He *started*? A dealer in quantity drugs?

SALAZAR: He's a fallible, corruptible human.

CASS: Well, he sure proved *that*.

SALAZAR: "We are every one frail. Consider none so frail as thyself."

CASS: Is that a Dead Sea Scroll thing?

SALAZAR: Thomas à Kempis. *The Imitation of Christ.*

CASS: Well yeah, man, because your boy better put some polish on his imitation . . . Look, you're impersonating a cop, and I'm impersonating a thief. Because I ain't a thief. This whole robbery incident just materialized. All by itself, like a dream. I figured as long as I'm in Houston and I'm kind of putting the fear in this woman, Kate Wendell, well, she's right here in the phone book. I'm dropping by. This had to do with my sister's job. Kate Wendell is my sister's boss. My sister is (*with feeling*) my—little—sister. My one and only sister. You got family?

SALAZAR: They're dead to me.

CASS: How'd they die? Wow. Like all at once they got killed?

SALAZAR: They're dead to *me*. To *me* they are dead.

Pause.

CASS: So I bang by, and here she comes to the door. "You Mrs. Wendell?" "Miss Wendell." "Okay. Miss." She's there with the guy, Jack. "Jack, look who's here." Because first of all before that I said to her, "Good evening, you homosexual maniac. I'm Marigold's big brother. We've spoken on the phone." And she says, "And in the Luby's cafeteria." I said, "You bitch. You lie. When I eat I sit down and order." So Jack turns up behind her and leans back his head with a bourbon or something in his hand and kills it off. He's going to deal with me. That's what people do, they finish their drink quick and deal with you. But another guy shows up behind him with a satchel and a gun. And this new guy stares at me. Looks a lot like Jack the boyfriend, could be related. He sets the satchel down, kind of confused. He's staring at me. He *shoots* the *gun*.

CASS *displays the holes in his shirt and the burn along his ribs.*

SALAZAR: He didn't mean to. That was Brother—

CASS: I kind of figured that. I didn't say he meant to. I think his nerves grabbed and boom—one of those events. So he set the gun down on the table and everybody stood around paralyzed for a little bit. Until suddenly I thought, Hey, I'm picking up this gun, and I'm grabbing your satchel here, and see you down the line I hope but not really. I mean, man, I was on a bender. I didn't remember this business till right now while I'm telling it. Now. Mr. Child of Jehovah. Listen. I got a question . . . I *do* wanna dialogue religion.

SALAZAR: What.

CASS: Could you maybe look upon me as an instrument of God?

SALAZAR: What?

CASS: If things happened, things that were done by me, things that you wish would have happened but you couldn't do it yourself—like when you've gotta put your dog down, man. But luckily he gets hit by a car. Otherwise you would've had to drag him out back of the house in the woods and shoot him, and wouldn't that bring you down, wouldn't that break your heart? Your dog was sick. I was innocently driving along. I ran over your dog for you. Now you're glad because finally he's dead.

SALAZAR: Is that how you feel about the woman who fell? The lovely Eldorado—

CASS: Fuck you! . . . I flushed your material down my toilet. I dissolved your drugs. They're oozing through the ecology right this second. The cotton's jumpin', and the fish are high.

SALAZAR: That's bad.

CASS: What's bad? It's *bad* for a so-called spiritual leader and he's the founder of his own group and they have even their own *vehicle* to be holding a satchel full of dope and trying to blow my ass up with a thirty-*eight*. In his friend's house! And he shouldn't have friends like her. What kind of substance was it, anyhow?

SALAZAR: I really don't have that information . . . I believe it was cocaine. (*Pause.*) I don't know how this happened. Her boyfriend set the whole thing up. He knows a dirty narc. Some lost soul in the DEA.

CASS: Jack set this up?

SALAZAR: Jack. And he's not Brother Jenks's brother. I believe he's brother to the Devil.

CASS: So—see? I *am* an instrument—an instrument of Jehovah.

SALAZAR: We, the Children of Jehovah . . . We are beginners . . . (*Pause.*) I don't know what possessed him! That Kate Wendell person! I just—can I tell you something?

CASS: Sure. Consider me—

SALAZAR: He came to me crying last night. Brother Jenks wept in my lap. Wept like a child in my lap. I just think he's always been in love with that woman.

CASS: She ain't that lovable.

SALAZAR: You asked for an explanation—

CASS: I didn't hear myself asking.

SALAZAR: *I* asked for an explanation. All right? I *prayed* for an explanation. She—and Jack Toast—are *evil*. And Brother Jenks is stuck loving her. Stuck! His heart is torn, he—

CASS: He'll get over that one. She is a *dog,* C of J.

SALAZAR: Our church is broke. We're finished. But the Lord . . .

Pause.

CASS: Did you push an FBI guy out of your car when it was in motion?

SALAZAR: Salazar? He got his jacket swiped. At the movies. (*Pause.*) There's so much putrescence! There's so much vile rot! Can you—

CASS: I'm an instrument!

SALAZAR: . . . Maybe.

CASS: I *told* you it was fate. I *told* you.

The phone rings.

Pause. SALAZAR *studies* CASS *silently.*

Staring at SALAZAR, CASS *grabs the phone in the middle of the fourth ring.*

As CASS *speaks, the two men stare at one another and the lights dim steadily.*

CASS: Hello . . . Franklin . . . Yes. (*Pause.*) Yeah, sure, definitely—

A long pause. SALAZAR *watches* CASS *raptly.*

Now, wait. I think you're trying to sell me a book, Franklin. That hurts my feelings, when you call me up and tell me your name and all, like we're going to be friends, and really you just want to sell me the *Famous Aviators* series . . . Because would you want me to do you that way too sometime, just when you need a friend? Because you know what? . . . I thought you were God . . . Just when you, you know—

Pause.

Franklin?

BLACKOUT

We hear him hang up softly in the dark.

SHOPPERS CARRIED BY ESCALATORS INTO THE FLAMES

A DRAMA IN TWO ACTS

Shoppers Carried by Escalators into the Flames was written for Campo Santo + Intersection and premiered at Intersection for the Arts (Deborah Cullinan, executive director) in San Francisco, California, on August 8, 2001.

Produced by Campo Santo (James Faerron, Margo Hall, Sean San Jose, Luis Saguar, Michael Torres, Drew Yerys; Denis Johnson: playwright in residence)

Cast

GRANDMA: Helen Shumaker
CASS: Sean San Jose
DAD: Michael Torres
TV: Brian Keith Russell
BRO: Luis Saguar
SUZANNE: Lisa Joffrey
GIB: John Polak
MARIGOLD: Alexis Lezin
PASTOR ROCK: Brian Keith Russell
MARCY: Catherine Castellanos
(The role of MARIGOLD was understudied and also performed by Gabriela Barragan)

Original musical score by Marcus Shelby
Additional music by Jim Roll

Designed by Suzanne Castillo, James Faerron, and Drew Yerys

Directed by Nancy Benjamin

Look, I am living. On What? Neither childhood
nor future grows any smaller . . .
— RAINER MARIA RILKE, NINTH DUINO ELEGY

GRANDMA: Around eighty

DAD: Around sixty

MARIGOLD: His daughter, late twenties

CASS: His youngest son; around thirty

BRO: The middle brother; mid-thirties

SUZANNE: Around thirty

GIB: Around thirty

PASTOR ROCK

MARCY: Mid-thirties

TV: A box full of voices

Scene: A lower-middle-income apartment in Ukiah, California, at the start of the third millennium

Set consists of two levels, separately lighted: the upper, DAD's bedroom; the lower, the kitchen/living room.

Players exit right, out the apartment's front door (which opens directly onto the outdoors), or left, into a hallway (which leads to GRANDMA's *room and also to the stairs up to* DAD's *bedroom).*

Sets and lighting should be simple and true-to-life; no music except as indicated. Let TV *be realistically rendered and inhabited by a live actor.*

Act I

SCENE 1

Downstairs at the Cassandra residence: kitchen-dining area; living area with a hide-a-bed couch, a recliner, a large TV *with its face turned upstage.*

GRANDMA *at the stove, the sink. Because she doesn't know where else to be. Making tea, washing dishes.*

In the living room sits her grandson MARK CASSANDRA, *called* CASS: *around thirty, in a Hawaiian shirt with a bullet hole in it; threadbare jeans; warped cowboy boots. Unshaven, unwashed.*

Both look down at a little barking dog we can't see but we sure can hear—indicated maybe just by one of those fifties-Disney-type elongated shadows on the wall. The dog is a Chihuahua. The bark is a yip.

DOG: Bark! bark! bark! bark! bark! bark! bark!

GRANDMA: Lord, look at her dribble. I don't like old people or old dogs or anything old like that.

CASS *jumps up and herds the tiny decrepit animal away from him with his toe.*

CASS: Dang! Ain't it housebroke *yet?*

GRANDMA: That dog is twenty years old. It should be killed . . . I'm going to make you some biscuits!

CASS: Grandma, I don't wanna stand in dog piss and hear about biscuits.

GRANDMA: Do you know what? Do you know what piss is? Urine.

She turns toward stove.

. . . With good white gravy! I'll make your mouth water, boy.

She opens and closes cupboards.

DOG (*outside*): Bark! bark! bark! bark!

CASS *adjusts a laminated Johnny Carson clock on the wall:*

CASS (*to Johnny Carson*): Sure, it's crazy. Did I say it wasn't? It's absurd. You're absurd.

GRANDMA: And popcorn!

She tosses a bag in the microwave.

Sporadic barking just outside the door.

CASS: Popcorn is absurd. (*Shifting to rapid:*) Okay, okay, okay, number one: I drank and I used and I'm like a (*shouting toward the barking*) DOG BEEN KICKED IN THE HEAD. Second I'm broke, number three I'm stuck here at Dad's house with Grandma, not to mention Dad himself, not to mention SHUT UP OR I WILL GODDAMN I PROMISE STEP ON YOUR HEAD ONE TIME.

Barking ceases.

GRANDMA: Boy, Jesus will forgive you that you talked to your grandmother thataway. But I believe I never will find it in my heart.

CASS: Have you got a cigarette?

GRANDMA: I don't smoke.

CASS *snags a butt from an ashtray.*

CASS: Would you have a match?

GRANDMA: Your ass and my face! . . . I mean my face, I mean, and your ass!

CASS *finds a lighter in a kitchen drawer.*

GRANDMA: I meant it the other way. *Your* face.

The popcorn takes off. The dog joins in. CASS *drags deep on his abbreviated smoke and steps out the front door.*

DOG: Bark! bark! bark! bark! bark! bark! YOWP!

GRANDMA *putters around, forgets herself, moves slowly to the recliner and eases herself into it, starts to speak, realizes she's alone. Her head lolls back, her mouth opens, she sleeps . . .*

BLACKOUT

Act I

SCENE 2

Lights up on GRANDMA *asleep in the recliner.* CASS *talks on the phone while eating popcorn. Dog's back inside, too.*

    CASS's *dad enters, carrying a bucket of Original Recipe chicken: a citizen of the Orbison-Presley type, with his white short sleeves rolled up two turns. He's just shaking loose a cigarette from his pack while setting down the chicken, but when he sees* CASS *he palms it and puts it back in his breast pocket along with the pack. Meanwhile:*

CASS (*on the phone*): Does she have—dang, she has a husband. Dang. Does that mean she's married? . . . Hey— (*Pause.*) I'm *fighting* to stay sober—I'm *fighting* to stay sober—uh. (*Pause.*) Yeah yeah, I'm *surrendering* to stay sober, I'm *surrendering* to stay sober— Wait—

DAD (*to* CASS): Is that long distance? (*Peers at* GRANDMA.) Have you given my mother drugs?

GRANDMA *wakes with a start.*

GRANDMA: Are my biscuits burning?

DAD: I've got biscuits right here.

CASS (*on the phone*): Can't I ask a low-key question about some girl without announcing we're engaged?

DAD: I saw the most remarkable thing just now.

GRANDMA: Did you? What was that?

DAD: It was a . . . tire.

GRANDMA: A tire.

DAD: I mean an inner tube.

GRANDMA: An inner tube. You saw a remarkable inner tube?

DAD: . . . Yes . . . I did.

CASS: Dad. Hi . . .

DAD: Cass. Back in Ukiah?

CASS: Uh—yeah . . . How's it going?

DAD: Oh, downhill to the river. Uphill after that. You know.

CASS (*on the phone*): I gotta go. Yeah. (*Hangs up.*) Can I stay here tonight, Dad?

DAD: Well, that all depends.

GRANDMA (*leaping up*): Don't you dare bring those biscuits in this house!

CASS (*to* DAD): I'm clean.

DAD: What about the booze?

CASS: Cross my heart.

GRANDMA (*heading for kitchen*): I'll make you some real biscuits! . . . It's six o'clock right now. Get the news! Get the
news about the shopping centers!

DAD (*assuming her chair and slowly taking out a thigh and sinking
his teeth into it*): I'll need some help here. Car washed, pick
up my suit at the cleaners, that sort of stuff.

CASS: Sure—

GRANDMA: The shopping centers are burning!

DAD *cuts* TV *on.*

TV: What does the busy professional need today? . . . What do
you care? You're not a busy professional.

DAD *hits the mute.*

DAD: And wear my suit to whatsername's wedding. May Jesus
bless her union even if it is the fourth or fifth.

CASS: Dad, are you getting more religious?

DAD: No. No.

The phone rings and DAD *sets his chicken aside.*

Dear Lord, let me answer as you would have me answer. Let
my words be your words—

CASS (*grabbing the phone*): Dad! God! . . . (*Into phone:*) No, ma'am, not me. Just passing through. Hang on—

DAD (*taking the phone*): I want you to take Grandma.

CASS: Take her where?

DAD: Hello? (*Pause.*) Jeanine. Yes. (*To* CASS:) To the wedding.

CASS: Whose wedding?

DAD: So-and-so's marrying your sister's old boy. Marigold's, you remember, the boy she—

CASS: Gib? Hightower?

GRANDMA: Gilbert Hightower. The love of your sister's life.

CASS: I wouldn't put it like that.

DAD (*on the phone*): Sure. Go ahead—Jeanine did you say? Explain away, Jeanine.

GRANDMA: And guess who—just guess—well, it's Suzanne Nash that he's marrying. Formerly Suzanne Cassandra, once upon a time. The love of your brother's life is marrying the love of your sister's life!

CASS: That's sick.

GRANDMA: Psh! Not here in California.

Meanwhile, CASS *tosses a bit of skin to the dog. He picks up the remote and points it at* TV.

TV: It's not good to feed your dog chicken. It's not good to insult your dog. It's not good. Shots of a beautiful Irish setter looking sad. Shots of a clown kissing a mongrel. It's never wise to—

DAD *signals:* TV's *too loud.*

CASS *punches the mute, sets down the remote, picks up the bucket of chicken. Meanwhile:*

DAD (*on the phone*): I see . . . What do you mean? Like Charles Lindbergh, or who?

GRANDMA: He called! Your brother called here this afternoon!

CASS: Bro?

GRANDMA: Yes! Luke called! I told him don't you dare come around here.

CASS: That ain't gonna stop him.

Throughout, GRANDMA *whips up dough, and* CASS *gets himself some milk and attacks the chicken at the dining room table.* GRANDMA *confiscates the store-bought biscuits.*

DAD (*on the phone*): Yeah, people like Charles Lindbergh. Like that woman who got lost—*Famous Aviators,* I understand. Did they ever find her? Amelia Earheart? (*Brief pause.*) I mean her bones, Jeanine, or the plane. What town are you

Famous Aviator people from, anyways? (*Brief pause.*) Jeanine, I'm not buying anything today, but just to be curious, how many volumes in the whole *Famous Aviators* series? (*Pause.*) Well, that's a pretty good value. I still don't want it. They've got shows for that now. They've got a whole History Channel. Uh, Jeanine: in some sense of it, I'm just wasting your valuable time on this discussion. To me time is no big deal, I'm semi-retired. I mean I could get the first one and send it back, or something, but—I could sign up and all just so you get a sale on your record. Just the first volume in the remarkable series. Just— (*Brief pause. He digs out his wallet.*) Well, you understand this is just to be doing you a favor. When the first volume gets here I intend to send it straight on back to the central people. I just want you to get the commission for now. Well, it's no big deal. Ain't going to cost me, and I'm just sitting here semi-retired on disability, watching the cavalcade of human existence. Kind of monitoring all that from a certain vantage point.

GRANDMA: The cavalcade of life! . . .

DAD: It's of a spinal nature, a spinal disability.

GRANDMA (*brandishing and tossing out fast-food biscuits*): This KFC dough is concocted in Mexico! They tie it up in giant plastic sacks and drive it everywhere in trucks!

DAD (*on the phone*): Oh, I get kind of kinked up and just lay there in bed sometimes. Like Elvis did toward the end. (*Brief pause.*) Nothing in particular. Nothing causes it, really. Just current events, for the most part, just the news of the times, it's so depressing. That's why I like the History Channel. (*Pause.*) What? (*Pause.*) Because it's history, Jeanine. It's all said and done. By other people. (*Pause.*) Yes I do. I have it ready. Visa card number five two three two, eight five two five, two aught three two, eight four one four, expires aught seven, thirty-one, aught three, in the name of Oliver Wendell Homes Cassandra: two L's at the end of Wendell, and Homes is H-O-M-E-S. (*Pause.*) Correct. Two. Double L. L plus L. (*Pause.*) No, it's a lot of names, but just one person.

He lowers the receiver and hangs his head. Pause.

DAD: God, it's incomprehensible. (*Pause.*) That there are voices out there with whole entire lives behind them, and . . . beautiful and strange . . . and—

CASS: Dad. Dad. Dad. Look at me. Dad?

DAD: Uh, yes.

CASS: Dad.

DAD: Yes, Cass.

CASS: A week at the most.

DAD: A week?

CASS: Can I flop here? Just a week at the outside. Can I stay?

DAD: Yes. Uh. Cass. Yes . . . love to have you.

GRANDMA *begins to sing.*
    DAD *sits quite still, listening.* CASS *stares outside.*

GRANDMA (*singing*):
    When they hung my handsome Daniel
    He looked so high surprised
    Gold fell from his pockets
    And a crow fell from the skies

    When they hung my handsome Daniel
    He looked so high surprised
    Although he'd watched the scaffold
    Since the twelfth day of July

    Although the judge passed sentence
    My handsome Dan must die
    Yet when the trapdoor opened
    He looked so flat surprised

    You should have seen his eyes

    My Daniel was so handsome
    You should have seen his eyes

Pause.

DAD: Well, the dog lived through another day.

Pause.

BLACKOUT

Act I

Lights low in the living room. Hide-a-bed folded out. CASS *alone: shaved and clean, a blanket wrapped around his midriff, hair slicked back and still wet from the shower: puttering around, looking for cigarettes, fiddling with the remote . . .*

TV: lonely lonely nights . . . lonely lonely nights . . . lonely lonely nights—

. . . the prehistoric evidence. They sift among the minute—

. . . here in the dark—

. . . the past—

. . . the limitless future—

There's nothing funny on. So quit pushing buttons.

CASS *hits the mute. Shouts upstairs:*

CASS: Daddy! Can I have a cigarette or not. (*Pause.*) Dad?

No answer. CASS *sighs, gets back in bed.*

Light tapping on the front door.

CASS: Uh . . . (*More tapping.*) Who's there?

BRO'S VOICE: Shhhhhh!

CASS: Who is it? Identify!

BRO'S VOICE: Shush, will you? Is she gone to bed?

CASS: Who is that? Bro?

CASS *wraps himself in his blanket, goes to the front door and cracks it.*

BRO: She asleep?

CASS: I guess.

BRO *tiptoes inside.*

BRO: I been standing out there the better part of an hour waiting for that maniacal old fossil's light to go out . . . How,
Tarzan.

CASS: You got a cigarette?

BRO: Not for every pitiful sumbitch wants one.

This is LUKE CASSANDRA, *called* BRO: *Bigger and beefier than*
CASS, *four years senior. He embraces his younger brother. Sits in the*
recliner while CASS *resumes the hide-a-bed.*
    They look each other over.

CASS: How goes it?

BRO: Oh, downhill to the river. (*Pause.*) Whatcha watchin'?

CASS: I don't know. The usual nonsense.

Pause. They regard the television. CASS *tries a couple channels, no sound.*

CASS: Where you been?

BRO: Redding, mostly.

CASS: Doing what?

BRO: Logging, mostly.

CASS: Ha!

BRO: Living with a retarded woman.

CASS: Uh . . . Now, you say, uh—

BRO: You say *ha,* I'm lying—okay, I ain't logging. I know what a log *is,* but I don't have the tiniest idea what you *do* with the goddamn things, I mean, what log-*ging* i-n-*gee* would be. I just say it. Really the last almost five years I been living with a retarded woman.

CASS: Yeah. Okay.

BRO: Yeah. North of Redding. She's got twenty acres and a house and all. I do everything around the place, kind of a hired hand who don't get paid. I steal from her. Small amounts.

CASS: Wow. Retarded? Well—so, uh—

BRO: And—I do screw her.

CASS: Well—

BRO: Yes, I do. Sometimes . . . I just haul off and screw her.

CASS: Oh my Lord.

BRO: She sort of seems to forget about it afterward.

CASS: Is it—mainly just you and her—?

BRO: Yep, just the two of us. It beats logging. (*Pause.*) I haven't seen you since before I got arrested that time. Where you been?

CASS: Me? Right here in Ukiah till a couple months ago.

BRO: Yeah? And then where?

CASS: I was back in Texas. Texas ain't there no more.

BRO: Shit. Did Mexico finally get it back?

CASS: What are you here for?

BRO: It's my town. Ukiah is *my* home.

CASS: What are you doing here? Is it the wedding?

BRO: I'm terrible.

CASS: You're going to the wedding?

BRO: I'll just sit there quietly.

CASS *hides his face and moans.*

BRO: She's the love of my life.

CASS: Do you even know her?

BRO: I was married to her. I was her first husband. Her first love. Her first lover. I was the first hombre to ride that little filly.

CASS: I mean . . . *now.* Hasn't it been about ten years since you two split up?

BRO: Eleven years. One-one. Pair of aces.

CASS: Split up after a lifelong union that lasted around two months?

BRO: June one to August thirty-one. Nineteen eighty-nine.

CASS: A legally binding summer romance.

BRO: It *is* a lifelong union.

CASS: Bro . . . Suzanne ain't much, you ask me.

BRO: She ain't perfect, but perfection is not the basis of what I'm talking about. I don't understand why I'm even discussing it with you. You'd hit eighteen in a blackjack game.

CASS: Yeah? You got witnesses?

BRO: You'd hit twenty-one. You'd hit blackjack if they let you. Ain't nothing perfect enough.

CASS: No, there ain't. Because look at your hands and your fingers and everything else. We are so . . . Feel your skin! We're made so . . .

BRO: So what.

CASS: So there.

BRO: Aaaaaah—

CASS: So beautifully. We should be turning over blackjack every deal. Nothing short of that is gonna do it. That's what we deserve is blackjack, blackjack, blackjack. I go along with Grandma on this one . . . Bro, I do. The most logical outcome of the whole enterprise is Heaven.

BRO: I like the way you stir around your concepts. You got the casino of the universe and the whole God-the-croupier thing. You always had the gift of gab.

CASS: I been on a strange journey through the desert wastes. Also the wetter part of Texas. A strange journey.

BRO: We oughta buy you some time on the religious channel. You know what's happening to you?

CASS: I'm trying to know.

BRO: You're turning into *him:* Dad. You are becoming Oliver Wendell Homes Cassandra.

CASS: Yeah. Dad's . . . upstairs.

BRO: Where is he? (*Pause.*) Really? Is he "upstairs"?

CASS: Yeah . . . Around sundown he was saying everything was beautiful.

BRO: "Beautiful, beautiful, beautiful . . . excuse me, everything's so beautiful I'm gonna put on these silver-tinted sunshades and spend three months in bed impersonating Roy Orbison." That's who you're turning into.

GRANDMA'S VOICE: Hon? Cass?

BRO: And meanwhile *Dad* is turning into *her.*

GRANDMA'S VOICE: Here you go, hon.

BRO: Jesus Christ.

BRO *hides behind the couch.*

BRO: Don't snitch me, boy.

GRANDMA *enters with* CASS'S *clothes clean and folded.*

GRANDMA: Warm from the dryer! (*As he dons his shirt:*) Are these your only clothes? Oh, Cass. Don't you have any others?

CASS: I got a box of stuff at my buddy's place. Bob Cornfield. He's a good old boy. He's my sponsor in the AA.

GRANDMA: Let's get the eleven o'clock news. Long as you're up. Are you up?

CASS: Up as long as you are, Grandma.

He hands her the remote.
   She settles into the recliner. CASS *gets his jockeys on, dressing under the blanket, and restocks the pockets of his pants with items he's kept on the arm of the hide-a-bed: pocket knife, notebook, wallet, etc. Meanwhile:*

GRANDMA: The Channel Four news. Pray they start with the political campaigns. If they start with the politicians, you know there's no big disasters to speak of. If they can't find anything more horrible to show you than some corrupt liar. If they start off with Jerry Brown especially. Oh! Goodness! Have you been drinking?

CASS: No, ma'am!

GRANDMA: Something smells like wine.

She puts her face in her hands very briefly and then raises it.

GRANDMA: What are we doing here?

Pause. CASS *snags a butt from the ashtray and gets it lit while:*

CASS: I'm waiting for a bed.

GRANDMA: Hon, you're on a bed. Wait no more.

CASS: A bed in rehab.

GRANDMA: Rehab? Rehab somewheres in Arabia? Rehab. (*Pause.*) Rehab in Persia?

CASS: Rehab on Idaho Avenue. The Starlight.

GRANDMA: The Starlight Motel?

CASS: The Starlight Recovery Center. They made it into a rehab.

GRANDMA: Who did? A-hab the A-rab?

DAD *enters from upstairs.*

DAD: What?

GRANDMA: He's going to Arabia on Idaho. At the Starlight.

DAD: You lost me. Who's stealing my Kools?

CASS: This is a butt.

DAD: It is now.

CASS: It was when I tuned it up, Boss. Ask Grandma.

GRANDMA: Give the poor feller one entire smoke. He's your boy and he's come home.

DAD: Home from where?

CASS: Well—home from down around home, Dad. I was back in Odessa a little while.

DAD: What was that like?

CASS: Nothin'. I didn't remember as much as I thought. It's just a place. Except the smells.

DAD: What smells?

CASS: Just everything. The smells kept taking my mind back to the past. (*Pause.*) And I was over in New Mexico some, just a week or so. Phoenix, Arizona ... Las Vegas, Nevada ...

DAD: Vegas. I sold my wedding ring in Las Vegas. My first one ...

CASS: What about hers?

DAD: Hers?

CASS: Do they let her keep her wedding ring in prison?

DAD: We're divorced.

CASS: *I* know.

DAD: So it stands to reason she's not married.

CASS: Well ... Yeah ...

DAD: And has no use for a wedding ring . . . I couldn't've married your stepmom if I wasn't divorced first.

CASS: And are you and Carol legally divorced now too? . . . So she ain't my stepmom, is she? Or is she? What's the rule on that?

GRANDMA: The *rule* is you don't go getting divorced! I never did! None of my people did, not originally. Then all of a sudden I don't know. Just California, I guess. From here it spread on out. The Vileness of California. The Vileness was spreading out, and we come a-headin' this way to collide with it, all of it. Idolators and UFOs and burning incense. Drive-up churches. Do you know what they call it? "Californication." Go down to State Street over by the courthouse, not a block from it, and you know what you'll see? The Divorce Store!

DAD: Momma, settle yourself.

GRANDMA: Oh my God, my holy Lord God Almighty. Did our Heavenly Father just spit on California and turn on his heel? I have not felt the touch of the sacred in my heart since we crossed that line into California . . . I've got to get out of here. I've got to *go,* I've got—

DAD (*overlapping*): Aw, Momma. . . . Will you make us some popcorn? Why don't you—I got you some of that that just pops in a sack in the microwave. Please, Momma, please—

GRANDMA (*overlapping*): I'm sorry. I'm sorry. I'm absolutely hysterical. Did you get some of that in the bag? Oh, well, I do think I'd like to give that a whirl. Let me get my reading glasses for the directions on the sack. Pop it in the sack! I don't mind if I do!

DAD (*overlapping*): Yes, Momma, sure thing, yes, Momma, yes, it pops automatically right in its own bag.

CASS: We tried it.

GRANDMA: We did! We tried it. That's true.

CASS: It was pretty good.

GRANDMA: It was. Cass liked it.

CASS: Yeah, it was pretty—

GRANDMA: But do you see this? Arthur Cassandra put this ring on my finger two weeks before my twenty-third birthday, and it has never been anywhere but right there where it is! I've never had it off!

DAD: Momma. Momma. Momma. (*Pause.*) I've still got my ring from Carol upstairs somewhere. It's got two diamonds in it. But I think they might be fake.

GRANDMA: Fake! That was your father's ring that I gave to you! Do you not remember? Oliver Wendell Homes Cassandra.

DAD: Oh, of course, of course, you're right, Momma, I apologize—

GRANDMA: He gave you your wedding ring for your second wedding, and he gave you your name after the greatest Chief Justice of the United States.

DAD: He misspelled it.

GRANDMA: The Chief Justice misspelled it.

DAD: It's his name. H-O-*L*-M-E-S. Not H-O-M-E-S.

GRANDMA: Dropping any old letter down in the middle. Your name is properly spelled. *His*—is a great big old total mess . . . Your father, Arthur Cassandra, was a champion speller, a gifted man just like you, a brilliant—he wrote campaign speeches for the Mayor of Odessa, Texas—Gus Willard. Your daddy loved poetry. He used to sit by your crib when we had it in the living room and read free verse by Walt Whitman . . . Walt Whitman was actually—a very *good* poet!

DAD: Gus Willard wasn't elected Mayor, Mother.

GRANDMA: He wasn't?

DAD: He lost the election by an impressive margin. The biggest ever.

GRANDMA: I knew him!

DAD: He was never the Mayor.

DAD *exits up the stairs.*

GRANDMA: I knew him! Every time I saw him and talked to him I believed I was seeing and talking to the Mayor!

She laughs.

Then later the ex-Mayor . . .

She sighs.

Don't ever get old, Grandson.

CASS: Very few are betting that I will.

GRANDMA: There's no percentage to the deal after a certain point . . .

CASS: Grandma, will you cut out the light? (*She does; lights very low now.*) Speaking of the past . . .

GRANDMA *sighs.*

CASS: Somewhere in here in this visit we better all sit around and talk out the past.

GRANDMA: The tragic side of life . . .

CASS: We have to deal with all that. Or some, anyways.

GRANDMA: That's what you said your *last* time around at the Starlight.

CASS: And did we deal with it? No.

GRANDMA: Yes!

CASS: No.

GRANDMA: *I* thought we did. It seems like we had enough of a powwow over it that your brothers both got in jail that night.

CASS: That's just our way of ducking the main thing. Get arrested.

GRANDMA: Huh! Talk sense!

CASS: I've had trained and certified counselors point that out to me, Grandma. More people escape *into* prison than ever escape *out*.

GRANDMA: Don't you let anybody tell you how to do like. You make up your own mind how you're going to be baptized and follow the Lord and don't get mixed up too deep in the Alcoholic Anonymous or the Narcotic Anonymous. "I am the way, the truth, and the light," sayeth Our Lord Jesus Christ. And anybody that don't clearly invoke his name is doing the work of the Devil Satan from down in Hell. That's from the Bible. Can your counselors go back in a time-travel device to Cherokee County, North Carolina? If they can't do that, then tell them to let me alone. It started to go bad when we all left Cherokee County.

CASS: I never left Cherokee County.

GRANDMA: Well, that's because you were never there.

CASS: I was never there. That's my point.

GRANDMA: Arthur Cassandra and I should never have made a move into Texas. The Nantahala Mountains will ever be my natural home.

CASS: Well, I'm from Texas as my home. You never should've brought us to California.

GRANDMA: I was brought same as you.

CASS: California made my mother crazy.

GRANDMA: Your mother never even got inside California.

CASS: Just the idea of it made her crazy.

Pause.

Don't cry, Grandma.

GRANDMA: I get through the days pretty good. I just don't like the nighttime. Why did Johnny go?

CASS: I don't know.

Pause.

GRANDMA: Jay Leno is all right, I don't mean to insult any-body. But I just don't like the nighttime anymore, and I never will. Actually, that Conan makes me laugh. He's just a little boy. But that's what's sad about him, he's just a boy, and it's so late at night.

CASS: The nights would go better if this family just talked a few things out.

GRANDMA: People don't like to get down and cut into all the monstrous things that's happened in a family. Scatter it all around and remember monstrous things.

CASS: Vehicular homicide ain't so monstrous.

GRANDMA: Say now, she wasn't dozing at the wheel. She bargained down from Murder in the First. We don't need to cut into the rot of all those things.

CASS: The rot's not in the things. It's in us.

GRANDMA *kisses his forehead.*

GRANDMA: Well, you've just got a verse for everything. You're the Living Bible.

Pause.

The *Most Wanted* show is on tomorrow night. I love that show. All day Saturday I look forward eagerly to *America's Most Wanted.* But then all day Sunday I just can't find anything on. Sundays are as long as Death Row . . .

CASS: There's plenty of sports. Sports that older people can enjoy. Senior people. Mature citizens. Like golf.

GRANDMA: Like golf?

CASS: Like tennis . . .

GRANDMA: But golf is so silly it makes my skin to crawl! It makes me ashamed and embarrassed just to think about golf. At least tennis is back and forth. Golf is just on and on over hill and dale like a man chasing a red-breasted robin! It just hops a little farther, and hops a little farther . . . and they're all too witless to give up chasing it. I wonder, did God Almighty invent golf to drive people away from the televisions so we'd spend Sunday afternoon with the Holy Bible? I watch the news on Sunday at five at night on Channel Four. Otherwise— Oh! Goodness! We're missing the news! Do you know how many underground shopping malls have burned up? Twenty-six underground shopping malls have *burnt*!

CASS: Is that true?

GRANDMA: Twenty-six!

BRO, *in his hiding place, can't stand it anymore.*

BRO (*behind the couch*): YOU'VE JUST SEEN THE SAME NEWS REPORT TWENTY-SIX TIMES, YOU SENILE OLD WOMAN.

GRANDMA (*after a fright*): I knew you were there!

BRO: No you didn't.

GRANDMA: Cass is going into the Starlight to get his drinking dried up. You should do the same. Unless it's me that stinks like cheap port. Good night, all.

BRO: Aaaah—

GRANDMA (*leaving*): No, it's fine, I've got a real good little TV in my room that don't sass its own grandmother LIKE A CONVICT.

Pause. CASS *thumbs the remote.* BRO *grabs it away.*

TV: —buried irretrievably at the bottom of the Sound. There were no survivors. Meanwhile, authorities declined to speculate as to—

BRO *hits the mute.*

BRO: What's the longest you been clean, Cass? And sober?

CASS: Ninety-seven days.

BRO: What's the shortest? Since you started with the AAA.

CASS: Thirty-two days.

BRO: And you've had several such glorious interludes of sparkling clarity.

CASS: What's it to you?

BRO: I'm your bro.

CASS: My ride is my ride. No need for your concern.

CASS *hit the remote.*

TV: *Am* I my brother's keeper? We plague ourselves with—

BRO *hits the mute.*

BRO: You are one wily little jit, ain't ya?

CASS: How do you mean?

BRO: You flop there at the Starlight a fortnight or two, no
worries, just long enough to get your lariat rolled up
round, and then back in the saddle. What is it—a sliding
fee scale?

CASS: What are you on?

BRO: What does it smell like I'm on?

CASS: Real real cheap wine.

BRO: That's what I'm on.

CASS: You always start talking like a regular cowpoke when
you get some shit in you.

BRO: Is it a sliding scale down there at the Starlight?

CASS: Yeah, podner.

BRO: They apply you for food stamps?

CASS: Sho nuf, cookie.

BRO: You end up paying, what—a hundred? Two hundred
bucks for a month of three hots and a cot?

CASS: Down at the Rawhide Ranchero.

BRO: What a racket. "I'm Cass. I'm an alcoholic." . . . You'll drink again.

CASS: You got a cigarette?

BRO: Nope.

CASS: I should be allowed to smoke a smoke. I ain't in jail.

BRO: I'm not forbidding you. I just don't got one. "Hi, Cass!" . . . You'll drink again.

CASS: Yes, I will. I plan to.

BRO: I said it first.

CASS: I intend to. The night before I go in there I intend to circumcise a giant jug of Cuervo and get piss-pants paralytic drunk.

BRO: Give you fifty bucks if you wanna make it tonight. It's my party.

BRO *takes off his shoe.*

I got a fifty-dollar bill right here in the bank.

He goes one-shoed to the fridge and attaches the fifty to it with one of those magnets.

A little froggy with a chef's hat on. Ain't that cute? . . . Cuervo Gold and the requisite groceries. Merely say the word.

CASS *plops down on the couch with a sigh.*
Pause while he sighs and sighs.

CASS: Bro? Before I go to the Starlight place.

BRO: Uh. Yes sir . . .

CASS: I have a list of things I'd like to deal with. You know, the family—the things—the family—

BRO: Aaaaaah . . . Hey. Dad spends his life in bed because he's depressed about losing his second wife. His second wife left him because he spent his life in bed all depressed over losing his first wife.

CASS: That's not what he says.

BRO: What does he say?

CASS: He says he has a bad back.

BRO: So he lies in bed watching TV for weeks at a time never moving.

CASS: He says the television inspires him . . . No, I don't buy it, course not, which is what I mean: we're all full of it up past our hairlines and we better get *honest*.

BRO: Aaaaaaaah—

CASS *yanks his pants off the floor and digs in a pocket. Meanwhile:*

CASS: I have a list. I've had this list since—I made this list over a year ago. It's part of a logically paced-out program of recovery. It's all got to be dealt with. People don't find the future till they wrestle it all out about the past. I put it all down in black and white. And then I got down to some serious procrastinating—I mean, it's been a year or better—but it was always right there. Right here. Look here at this notebook. I've had it with me a solid year in my back pocket.

BRO: Better change your britches. Whoa! Here come the actual britches themselves!

CASS: I've got just a few things. A page for each thing. See? Each thing on its page. See?

BRO: Aaaaaah—aaaaaah—I don't have to see. I know what it is. "Why is Dad so depressed?" "Why did Mom—" Aaah. Piss on that shit.

CASS: Good. Good! It's happening! We're doing it!

BRO: Good! I can clear this all up for you in about eight seconds. Dad's depressed because Mom ran over the baby. Mom ran over the baby because—

CASS: By accident! Sure, I know, but—

BRO: Accident?

CASS: Yeah. I mean, okay, maybe—

BRO: Ask John. He remembers.

CASS: I remember, too.

BRO: You were four. I was nine. John was thirteen.

CASS: Marigold is the only one who can't remember.

BRO: Marigold!

CASS: She was only one and a half.

BRO: Marigold wouldn't remember even if she could. She'd refuse to remember even if it was burned on her brain. Don't you understand yet about Marigold?

CASS: She was only one and a half.

BRO: The thing to understand about Marigold is she remembers everything. Especially the stuff she's forgotten. Especially that stuff. Don't get me started about Marigold.

CASS: You started all by yourself.

BRO: Don't get me started about Marigold. I could write a book. I was there, and I remember. Mom was intending to run over us all.

CASS: We disagree about that.

BRO: One by one.

CASS: I disagree.

BRO: So—all at the same time?

CASS: Okay, maybe *you* say—

BRO: She put little Amy on the ground there, on the pave-
ment, and very calmly proceeded—or really hysterically,
psychotically out of her mind proceeded—hysterically but
deliberately—proceeded to run over the baby's head.
Wouldn't you be depressed if your wife did that? Hey.
Hey. Well? Wouldn't you be depressed if your wife did
that, Cass?

CASS: *If*—

BRO: And wouldn't you be fucked up if your mother did that?

CASS: *If*—

BRO: If—

CASS: Yeah—

BRO: Well, she did. And he is depressed. And we are fucked
up. (*Pause.*) I don't mind it. I enjoy it.

He hits the remote.

TV: The commissioner points out that since 1994, twenty-six
underground shopping malls around the globe have suf-
fered fires which he describes as quite similar in nature.

BRO: Yeah: they're hot in nature. When you hot, you hot.

TV: Or for instance . . . McDonald's is nice. This might be just the time for one of those extremely tasty burgers.

BRO: I ate.

TV: But nothing will ever again taste like it did when you were a child.

BRO: You're one of them *new* goddamn TVs.

TV: I love the play area for the kiddies. I'd love to swim around in that pool of plastic spheres. It's so elemental. I'd love to buy an enormous lipstick-red eighteen-and-one-half-foot-long Cadillac Eldorado convertible and drive it right into that pool of plastic balls. Can you imagine it? Everybody would say, "Look at that *colossal* Zenith TV driving that lovely Eldorado convertible into that sea of many-colored orbs!"

BRO: You ain't so colossal.

TV: Would you like me to show you footage of your mother in Odessa, Texas, 1976? (*Imitating sounds and voices:*) SCREEEECH . . . She jumps from her Impala, bawling at her children: "I've had it! Had it! Had it!"

BRO AND CASS (*watching*): No, Mom! No! No! No! Mommy!

TV: "I'm gonna kill you . . . I'm gonna put you on the ground and run over you! . . . Every one of you, I'm gonna make your fucking head like a fucking tortilla!"

BRO AND CASS: Mommy! No! Stop it! Mommy!

TV: "Waaaaa!" Vrooom vrooom VRRROOOOM!!!
"WWWAAAA—" *skreek!*

Silence. The brothers stare in horror. A pause as they gradually recover.

CASS: Okay.

BRO: Okay.

CASS: She said she was going to, but I don't think she woulda
done it.

BRO: Well, tell it to little Amy.

CASS: Little Amy. Little with the flat head. And no blood. To
speak of. Just a tiny little bit around her eyes and some
from just one ear.

BRO: Yeah, is that how you remember it? Me too.

CASS: Her brains didn't come out or anything. Her skull
didn't pop, nothin' like that. Her head just got real flat
sideways, like a fish's head.

BRO: Because she was a baby.

CASS: What?

BRO: Their bones are quite a bit softer than ours.

CASS: When was the last time you saw her?

BRO: Me? Right then. Right there—when the EMTs loaded her up.

CASS: I mean Mommy.

BRO: Oh. Her? I was around—I guess I was eleven or so. Years before we come out here. Grammaw would've taken us to visit her any time we wanted, just about, but . . . (*Shrugs.*) We quit visiting.

CASS: It's funny. We talk about her like she's Mommy, she's real, but there she is in Gatesville, Texas, two days away by Greyhound—only you don't wanna go visit her because it wouldn't make any sense. It ain't her. And it isn't even us. It's nobody. There's just these real sick memories all over us like stink. These memories that belong to non-existent people. It isn't reasonable nor fair.

BRO: You know her name was actually Amiga.

CASS: Amy. Yeah. Course I knew that. Amiga.

BRO: When somebody puts a name like that to a child—that's a textbook symptom right there. Any clinical psychologist could tell you, sure as shit: there's going to be an incident.

CASS: Why are you so *full*—of *nothin'* . . .

BRO: Well? Look at the order of the names: John, Luke, Mark, Marigold, Amiga. Regular, regular, regular, kind of bizarre, then pee-sychotic.

Pause.

TV:

> —towering speed my lipstick Cadillac,
> my crazy, my red-as-hell convertible,
> my blazing baboon's-ass-red Eldorado
>
> I drive past exit after exit like
> A bullet shining. Desert take me. Desert
> break my bones.

I am going through snow in my convertible with the top down. I am going through rain. I am going through a cloud of moths. I am going through a hall of mirrors, an infinite confusion of reflected red Eldorados. I am nobaddy's facking mather!

BRO (*slapping at* TV): Man—man—

TV: Violence? You wanna threaten *me* with violence? I am the everlasting *God* of violence, pal.

BRO (*slapping* TV): Man—she drove—an *Impala*.

Pause.

We hear sounds outside: A car's door opens and slams several times. Meanwhile:

HE OUTSIDE: Don't get in the car. (*Slam.*) Don't get in the car. (*Slam.*) Don't even—don't do it. (*Slam.*) You are not getting in. Don't do it. (*Slam.*)

SHE OUTSIDE (*simultaneously*): I'm getting in the car. (*Door opens.*) I'm getting in the car. (—*Opens.*) I'm getting in. (—*Opens.*) I'm getting in.

CASS (*looking out*): Well just git in it and *drive,* and ye shall be healed . . . A brand-new Camaro. Oh you nasty. Boy I'll bet them things is *quick.*

(*The dialogue outside overlaps:* "Don't do it—" "Don't boss me—")

BRO: What is it, a Camaro?

CASS: A dirty filthy nasty sexy Camaro. Brand new . . . And guess whose? (*Turning to* BRO:) I hope they got cigarettes!

BRO: Who is it?

CASS: Just some people; visitors . . . just the love of your life. Also accompanied by the love of *her* life.

BRO: Yer goofin'—! Turn out the light.

Doorbell rings. Pause.

CASS AND BRO: Who is it? Who's there?

GIB'S VOICE: It's Gib.

SUZANNE'S VOICE: It's Gilbert Hightower.

BRO (*whispering*): Turn out the light.

GIB'S VOICE: And Suzanne.

CASS *prepares to answer the door, jamming his pants on.*

BRO (*whispering*): Cut the light out!

CASS: What? No.

BRO (*menacing hiss*): Turn it *out* . . . Not the porch light! Keep the porch light on!

CASS *cuts the lights, all but the muted* TV.

BRO: The TV! The TV, too!

TV (*as* CASS *approaches*): Please don't. Please. Please don't—

BLACKOUT

BRO (*whispering in the dark*): Okay!

A *pinpoint light hits two bare buttocks upraised about waist-level.*
    We hear the front door opening. Light from porch now as GIB *and* SUZANNE *enter.*
    BRO *crouches on the hide-a-bed with his pants down, postured like the center in a football game just before the hike, his butt jutting over the back of the divan.*

The couple get quite a jolt from the sight. Lights up as CASS *hits the switch.*

CASS: Hi!—uh—damn! The dog's back indoors! Hey! . . . Gib, uh, Suzanne—damn you little critter—

DOG: Bark! bark! bark!

GIB *recovers first, addressing* CASS *while* BRO *tumbles off the couch and fixes his trousers and spreads his arms for their consideration.*

Pause.

GIB: What is that little Chihuahua dog's name?

CASS: Nobody knows. Maybe Dad knows. I don't know.

He feints after the dog. Dog gets under the couch and quiets down. Then:

GIB (*to* CASS): Back in Ukiah!

CASS: Yep. That's the impression everybody's getting.

SUZANNE: Actually we knew that. We heard.

CASS: News travels like its ass was on fire.

GIB: Well, you spoke to Carl on the phone, and he quickly got on the phone to me.

SUZANNE (*to* BRO): Luke—

BRO: Bro.

GIB: We had no idea *you* were here, Luke.

BRO *and* SUZANNE *stare at each other.*

BRO: I'm not here in any verbal sense.

He leaves the room.

SUZANNE: What did he mean by that?

GIB: I'm not his translator.

CASS: I think he means he's not talking to anybody these days. In other words he ain't verbal.

GRANDMA'S VOICE (*from her room*): Don't you dare! Luke! You were not raised to ransack people's quarters!

CASS *exits toward the voices, leaving* GIB *and* SUZANNE *alone. They embrace. She caresses his crotch.*

SUZANNE: Wow, you got a nice pancho packed with wowsers!

GIB: You make me crazy.

She kisses him hungrily. He draws back.

GIB: This is all about his butt, isn't it?

Voices off distract them:

GRANDMA'S VOICE: Come back here with that thirty-two, young feller! . . . That's a lady's gun!

BRO *enters,* CASS *following.*

GIB: What gun?

GRANDMA *comes in, too.*

GRANDMA: Hi! It's the newlyweds! The soon-to-be's, I mean to say.

SUZANNE: Good evening, Mrs. Cassandra.

GIB: What . . . gun.

GRANDMA: Now, listen. If you each of you just *decide,* with your *mind, each* of you, to give more than you get, you'll be a blessing to each other forever.

GIB: Uh . . .

GRANDMA: Forever!

GIB: Thank you.

GRANDMA: It's that simple.

GIB AND SUZANNE: Thanks. Thank you.

GRANDMA: You hear me?

GIB AND SUZANNE: Sure. Yes, thank you—

GRANDMA: That's all you need to know.

CASS: I owe you guys a present, huh? I just got back to town—

GRANDMA: Mark my words! I'm old! I know my stuff!

GIB AND SUZANNE: Thanks. Okay. No problem . . .

CASS: I'm kinda, you know—working something up—

SUZANNE: Actually, we came to disinvite you.

CASS: Disinvite me?

GIB: You weren't invited.

BRO: Suzu—

SUZANNE: Suzanne.

BRO: Was *I* invited? Suzu?

GIB: Hell, no.

SUZANNE: How could we invite you or not invite you? We didn't even know where you were.

BRO: Okay. But under the new conditions—

SUZANNE: As far as we knew, *nobody* knew.

GIB: No. You're not invited.

BRO: —under the new, improved circumstances—(*Dog starts barking.*)—that is, with me actually *here* now—Shut *up,* will you?

DOG: Bark! bark! bark! bark! bark! bark! bark! bark! bark! bark!

GIB (*turning on the dog*): Yeah! The little Chihuahua dog's going to make a speech! (*Dog quiets.*)

Meanwhile BRO *draws a small revolver from his pants pocket and aims it at the back of* GIB's *neck.*

GIB: How old exactly is that little Chihuahua dog anyways?

Nobody answers.
   GIB *turns around and finds the gun pointed at his nose. Pause.*

GIB: Aw . . . this is too trailer-park for me.

BRO: I thought you lived in a trailer park.

GIB: We live in the Trails Park Subdivision. A community of very nicely constructed homes. We have a basement.

BRO: Am I supposed to start burning with envy?

For a couple seconds they're distracted by GRANDMA, *who heads for the kitchen area.*

BRO: Grandma—

GRANDMA: What, Luke?

BRO: What is the deal?

GRANDMA: Well, I'm thinking some microwave popcorn and whatever you all would—

BRO: Damn. Hey. (*As* CASS *hits the remote and turns on* TV:) Hey!

TV: The president has called for calm. He met this afternoon in the Oval Office with advisors from—

BRO: *Hey!*

CASS *hits the mute.*

BRO: I am creating an *atmosphere.*

Pause.

GIB: Cass, will you talk to him?

CASS: About what?

GIB: About what he's *doing* with a *gun.* And about—whatever it is—*not* doing it.

SUZANNE: Because you're the one who can talk to him.

BRO (*to* SUZANNE): You always could talk to me pretty good.

TV: Let's all settle down. Stay tuned for *Late Night with Conan O'Brien*. (BRO *points the gun at* TV.) I'm not talking. (BRO *thumbs back the hammer.*) Sorry. Sorry. Sorry.

GRANDMA: It's not loaded.

TV: I knew that. Go ahead. Do your worst. (*As popcorn takes off:*) Popcorn, anyone?

SUZANNE: That's one of those new tvs!

BRO *yanks the trigger and the gun goes off and* TV *explodes. Everybody shouts and the dog says yeow-wow!*

BRO: GOD! Sorry! Sorry! Sorry sorry sorry. *Gram*maw! . . . Aaaaaah . . . (*To* SUZANNE:) When you wouldn't take me back it made me want to binge on whiskey till my liver quit.

GIB: When was *this*? Did you—did he contact you?

SUZANNE: Gib. I think— Well, he wrote a letter . . .

CASS *pries the gun from* BRO's *fingers, unloads it, places gun and bullets on counter in kitchen. Meanwhile:*

BRO: I wrote, I phoned, I did every damn thing, and now I'm here to be at the wedding.

GIB: You won't be.

BRO: I been ringing your phone off the hook at the Trails Park trailer park. Talking to your machine.

GIB: And did she answer? Did you answer? And get it straight, it's not a trailer park. I wouldn't put her in one. Did she answer is all I want to know.

SUZANNE: No! I— No I did not!

GIB: You just said five minutes ago you didn't know where he was—

SUZANNE: I didn't want to muddy the waters, Gib.

GIB: You thought you'd keep things *clear*. By covering things *up*.

BRO: Suzu, Suzu—

SUZANNE: Su-*zanne*—

GIB: HALT! CEASE FIRE! (*Pause.*) Let me just go over the not-invited list. *You* are not invited, and *you* are not invited, and *you* are not invited—to my wedding. Over and out. (*To* SUZANNE:) You are still invited.

SUZANNE: Thanks.

GIB: But we're rapidly getting to where I really don't give a shit.

SUZANNE: Look, I love you.

GIB: Did you say "Luke, I love you"?

SUZANNE: "Look"! "Look"! Not "Luke"! I love *you*.

GIB: You're *faking*. I can tell you're faking. The minute you laid eyes on him you went all fake on me.

BRO: See? Other people can see it.

GIB: Do you know what? . . . Where's the damn phone book!

He starts searching.

BRO (*to* SUZANNE): We made something that— Okay!

CASS (*prompting him*): What you're doing here is important—

GIB: Listen, Simple: will you butt out?

BRO: Yeah, and it's so long ago I can hardly feel it, and you can hardly feel it—but it's like a structure that . . . contains us, and—

SUZANNE: Structure.

BRO: Kind of like monkey bars.

CASS: Kind of like a cage.

BRO: *No*—you can climb *around* on them.

SUZANNE: Kind of like a monkey.

BRO: —and I don't think we should just wreck it.

SUZANNE: It's the past, the past, you're only talking about the past! . . . You're talking about the past like it was a thing, but it's gone, it's not a thing, it's not a thing, it's nothing.

CASS: The! Past! Let's deal with it. We gotta deal with it.

BRO: How do we deal with it? Blot it out, is all! Make it disappear!

GRANDMA: Time travel!

CASS: We do something positive! We join an organization—

BRO: Jesus Christ! An organization!

GRANDMA: (*overlapping*): I don't think I want to join an organization, Cass—

BRO: (*overlapping*): *What* "organization"?

CASS: Something like Mothers Against—Vehicular Homicide or—the *point* is—

BRO: Mothers, Against, Vehicular, Homicide.

CASS: You help others, is the idea, turn your tragedy into your launching pad . . .

BRO: Turn your—! I'm not gonna repeat that phrasing even just to ridicule it.

CASS: Blot it out then! Blot out the past! Lay up in bed—travel in time—drink it away . . . Where have you been the last going on five years? Nowhere! Dreaming about the olden days with little Suzu! And you? And you! The past blotted *you* out! The past wins!

GIB: WHAMMO PRESTO.

GIB *grabs the phone from the kitchen counter and holds it overhead with both hands. He starts punching buttons.*

GRANDMA: Who's he calling now? The police I hope.

GIB: Hello, Mrs.—can I speak to Pastor Rock please?

SUZANNE: What are you calling the Pastor for?

GIB: Why? Because tonight is the night! (*Into phone:*) Pastor Rock?

GRANDMA: A pastor! . . . Tell him this family needs a miracle.

GIB: Pastor Rock, I'm very sorry to be so late and probably, you know, waking you up. (*Pause.*) This is Gib Hightower, me and Suzanne Nash are your wedding for Sunday. (*Pause.*) Yessir. (*Pause.*) I haven't gone to church much, I'm the first one to admit. (*Pause.*) Well, if you mean your particular church, Pastor, I guess not at all. But I have a situation I'd like to get some very serious help on here. I'm saying I'm about to ask you to go considerably out of your way and—this is something I need tonight, Pastor Rock.

GRANDMA (*into phone, over* GIB's *shoulder*): WE NEED A MIRACLE!

BRO (*to* SUZANNE): I'm just asking for a little acknowledgment.

GIB (*hanging up phone, grabbing* SUZANNE's *hand*): Suzanne. You're coming with me.

SUZANNE: Where?

BRO: Where? Yeah!

GIB: I'm going to get Pastor Rock. He's reluctant. I'll convince him face-to-face. (*Pause.*) I'm gonna bring him back here and marry this woman under your nose.

BRO: I thought I was dis-invited.

SUZANNE: Gib—?

GIB: We're dis-inviting everybody else!

As GIB *hauls her toward the door,* CASS *grabs his boots.*

CASS: I'll catch a ride as far as the highway.

GRANDMA: Where are *you* going this time of night?

CASS *grabs the fifty off the fridge and waves it high.*

CASS: Shopping!

BRO *whoops.*

CASS, SUZANNE, *and* GIB *exit door fast.* GRANDMA *stands facing door after it shuts.*

GRANDMA: WE NEED A GODDAMN MIRACLE!

BRO *keeps whooping.*

BLACKOUT

Act II

SCENE 1

Upstairs at the Cassandra residence, built over the living room.

A dark bedroom like a mausoleum. A nightstand, a darkened lamp, a glass of water. Flickering light from TV. TV *plays the theme from* Looney Tunes *or some such happy music.*

On the wall above the bed a large iridescent-on-velvet portrait of Elvis Presley singing or a Polynesian woman with naked breasts or something like that.

Throughout the scene, the atmosphere is hushed and holy.

Dad lies out straight under the covers, propped up on pillows. He wears dark sunglasses.

He's watching TV: *Laugh track. He moves. Laughter. Shifts. Laughter. Puts his face in his hands and weeps. Laughter. Sighs. Laughter.*

He raises the remote . . . hits the channel button repeatedly.

TV: Now is the time for all good men to come to the aid of
   their country—

   —expecting a miracle—

   —(*Singing:*) We're all existin' on the same planet
   We're all inhabiting the ball
   Ain't it ironical
   That it ain't conical
   Or some of us would surely fall

   Your wife put Amy's head beneath the wheel
   And acted out her black psychotic rage

That's why your second wife left you
And rode off on her wooden steed
And drifted off among the buttercups
And left you here to rot and bleed

DAD *hits the remote repeatedly.*

TV: Shots of a skiing competition: sunshine, excitement, colors
bright against the snow . . .

Then images of a burned-out shopping mall: water drib-
bling over charred and melted *stuff* . . .

Miss America, and splashing fireworks, and flowers waving
in a field . . .

Then the same shopping center, only now a blazing inferno.
People flee in panic. In the foreground is none other than
you yourself, Oliver Wendell Homes Cassandra, dressed
just as we see you in the flesh right now in your comical
pajamas. Your eyes are wide, your mouth wide open. You
explode into flames.

Meanwhile, MARIGOLD *enters.*
She comes in cautiously. Sits on the edge of the bed. For a long time
DAD *fails to acknowledge.*

TV: —twenty-eighth sign, or symptom, is one which family
members may not be quick to notice. You take long aimless
walks. You drive the less inhabited roads all night, without
a destination, listening to voices on the AM radio. When

you see long-haul trucks in the distance, so far ahead of you down the road you can't hear the noise they make, silent trucks floating away from you toward the horizon, you ache unbearably with—

—Survivors of last month's blaze, the worst in New Jersey history, told stories of mannequins afire and gift-wrapped packages bursting into flames—

DAD: (*hitting the mute*): Burnt-up gifts. Think what a disappointment that would be.

MARIGOLD: Dad? Can you see me? . . . It's me. Marigold.

DAD: Hello, Marigold.

MARIGOLD: Hi.

DAD: Would you be real?

MARIGOLD: Yes, Dad. I'm just on suspension.

DAD: . . . I'm not sure I comprehend.

MARIGOLD: I mean from work. The Department. You knew about that.

DAD: The Police Department?

MARIGOLD: I'm not in the Police Department, Daddy. I'm in the Department of Agriculture.

DAD: "Agriculture" . . . Words get destroyed in my mouth. They come out meaningless. I can't believe how dishonest I've become. Words in my mouth are like tiny, whole lives destroyed by a giant.

My every thought is like a crumbling rock,
it just gives way beneath my mind
and my mind stumbles and staggers downward dragging
my soul along with it . . .

I went to the cleaners to get my suit. Just as I was about fifty feet from the door, you know the cleaners over there in the shopping center, I saw a dress going toward it, a woman's pink dress suit, entirely by itself. Because of the angle and some cars in the parking lot that's all I saw, an empty dress drifting toward the dry-cleaning establishment. (*Pause.*) Nobody carrying it. A pink dress like the ghost of a cartoon . . . (*Pause.*)

Back in town?

MARIGOLD: Dad?

DAD: I'm thinking of every sad thing in the world.

MARIGOLD: Dad, could you take off your sunglasses?

DAD: Yes. Quick as I get a couple things figured out.

Pause.

I'm trying to figure out everything I saw between now and the last time I was in bed.

MARIGOLD: You mean yesterday.

DAD: Everything I saw. I feel it reaching for me. Everything's got something to say.

A black rubber inner tube—two yards in diameter at least, standing up straight on its rim, tall as a man, just rolling along the street. Rolling right past this apartment house. Not a soul in sight. Five o'clock in the afternoon. Nothing else moving anywhere around here. Not a sound in the world but the wind. Big old inexplicable inner tube rolling by like it had a select purpose.

    Then up the street I see three little schoolboys all out of breath, chasing toward me. When they reach me they give up. There goes the inner tube. It's still just rolling along. The wind's got it somehow. It enters State Street without observing the stop sign. A black pickup strikes it dead-on, and it goes sailing up into the air and over behind some bushes in front of the public library . . . I'm holding a bucket of fried chicken, got my arm around this bucket of fried chicken like a little child . . . (*Pause.*) That's what I have to deal with right now. Among other things.

Pause.

MARIGOLD: I flew from Houston to SFO and rented a car.

DAD: SFO?

MARIGOLD: Yes, Daddy. The City. San Francisco.

DAD: That what they're calling it these days?

MARIGOLD: They've always called it that, Daddy.

DAD *removes his sunshades and peers at her.*

   Pause.

DAD: What's the O for?

MARIGOLD: I don't know.

DAD: Oh. Oh yeah. OK . . . Oh my soul. It *is* my soul. It's my
   darlin' Marigold. Oh, baby. I thought you were here about
   the gunfire. I thought you were the police.

They embrace.

MARIGOLD: There's a kind of situation, Daddy. I've been dele-
   gated to tell you Bro humbly apologizes for ruining the TV.

DAD: Yes. I thought I heard his voice. Are the police here yet?

MARIGOLD: No. Was he shooting?

DAD: I believe it was just that thirty-two of Mother's. It wasn't
   all that loud . . . Are you still on the forced vacation?

MARIGOLD: I'm on suspension from the Department.

DAD: Yes. What was it?

MARIGOLD: Four weeks this time. Now it's two weeks—two weeks left.

DAD: I meant the reason.

MARIGOLD: But they'll extend it another four weeks, I think, because I'm uncooperative.

DAD: And there's the reason. The Cassandra pride. Well, that's always the reason for everything we do, I guess. Did Bro actually say to you that he was sorry?

MARIGOLD: No. We didn't talk. He's asleep in a chair. Napping.

DAD: Dreaming he's sorry.

MARIGOLD: Anyway, things are quiet. Grandma's in bed, probably watching one of her talk shows.

DAD: I can't watch talk shows. The conversations make me tense inside. I'm so afraid they'll stall out and just . . . stare.

MARIGOLD: They were shooting a gun? You actually heard a shot? Or shots?

DAD: Nothing to get involved in.

Pause.

Marigold? Do you have any tattoos?

MARIGOLD: Me? No . . . Tattoos?

DAD: And there's the chief symptom. Not one tattoo among all of us. We're too prideful . . . Do you see? Nothing's good enough for us. No tattoos . . . Nothing can be permanent because the next thing's got to be new and improved. We live around the next curve in the road. We're never *here,* nothing's finished, it's never the end.

MARIGOLD: Well, but you got married—that's sort of permanent—and Bro—and—at least it's *decisive* to get married—

DAD: Marriage . . . We'll get married, but we never mean it. Our unions are the erasable variety. John, Luke, and I were all in the service. Three enlisted men. A total of nine years in the ranks, and not a single tiny tattoo amongst us.

MARIGOLD: But Cass has quite a number of tattoos.

Pause.

DAD: Tattoos?

Pause.

And he was never *in* the service . . .

He sighs.

Sad! Beautiful! Beautiful! Sad!

MARIGOLD: Daddy, it's depression. They have . . . *excellent* medication for depressed—

DAD: You can't medicate the backbone blues.

MARIGOLD: I know, Daddy. But John's been taking some, and he feels great. Or much better.

DAD: John? Whenever did you see John?

MARIGOLD: He calls me sometimes. Just out of the blue. I don't know where he's, you know, hiding—

DAD: The last time I saw John was right there on that television: up on the roof of the parking ramp in downtown Dallas. On the news. Shooting down into the street . . . holding a phone to his left ear and a revolver to the other. Holding himself hostage. Demanding a jug of wine. Enjoying the natural freedom of an idiot . . . He's been tried and sentenced in absentia. Eight years minimum when they catch him. As they surely will. Anybody with his brand of thought processes . . .

Pause.

I remember being a little girl I never was.

Pause.

When your brother John . . . Oh.

Pause.

Oh. John's been caught, you know.

MARIGOLD: He has?

DAD: Yes, in the strangest place. Iowa.

MARIGOLD: He has?

DAD: Yes, darlin'. Darlin' Marigold. Or Ohio. His lawyer
called from Dallas to say he'd been contacted but regretted
he couldn't be of help in this case because he's a district
attorney now and was actually the one who filed the request
for extradition. But anyway he says that John is in Iowa or
Ohio awaiting extradition. Or possibly Idaho. Ask your
grandmother about it. She's got all the details. They're very
tough in places like Iowa. The travel arrangements are
pretty doggone medieval.

MARIGOLD: I — Dad . . . Daddy, didn't you tell anybody yet? I
was downstairs, I came in, I— nobody said a word about it.

DAD: Your grandmother was the one the lawyer actually talked
to. I get stuff secondhand. I get stuff secondhand, and then
I turn it all over endlessly in my mind . . .

Pause.

I guess you'll be at the wedding.

MARIGOLD: Gib and Suzanne? I think it's just for the imme-
diate family.

DAD: It seems to have a wider attraction.

MARIGOLD: Looks like you've got a full house.

DAD: It's crowded. I'm not comfortable outside this room.

MARIGOLD: Cass has dibs on the couch. Maybe I'll stay at the Lu Anne Motel.

DAD: But the Lu Anne Motel is gone, honey.

MARIGOLD: Oh . . .

DAD: It's gone. I think they moved it to Dallas or someplace like that.

MARIGOLD: Oh . . . And the Starlight's gone . . .

DAD: Why didn't Grandma tell us you were coming?

MARIGOLD: Grandma didn't know, Dad.

DAD: Grandma always knows. Doesn't she?

MARIGOLD: Usually.

DAD: Does she know why you came home?

MARIGOLD: I'm on suspension.

DAD: Don't get me wrong. I'm glad you came.

MARIGOLD: When they put you on suspension—you really feel suspended . . . yanked up by the suspenders . . . dangling . . . in suspense . . . in suspended animation.

DAD: I can see you've given the experience some thought.

MARIGOLD: And when I'm not suspended, I travel too much. I've got no pets, no houseplants. The only other living things in my life is the stuff in my refrigerator, and when I finally come home it's always rotten.

Pause.

I mean . . .

DAD: I know. Oh well.

Pause.

MARIGOLD: Daddy, do you remember that peacock we had? Paco?

DAD: Yes. Pepe. Or Pancho.

MARIGOLD: Paco.

DAD: Paco. He was beautiful.

MARIGOLD: He was.

DAD: And he was psychopathic.

MARIGOLD: No! He was just—sort of a little—

DAD: I've never seen any winged creature behave that way. He'd put his head down and charge straight into the side of the coop. Ram the chicken coop like a bull. A psychopathic peacock.

MARIGOLD: I can still smell the stink of those hens. I loved collecting the eggs from the roosts. Every egg I found I couldn't have been happier if it was gold . . . Daddy, was I the only one who felt that way?

DAD: About eggs?

MARIGOLD: About the eggs. About Paco, and the chickens: about the farm. That it was golden.

DAD: It wasn't a farm. It was an acreage.

MARIGOLD: That it was golden.

DAD: An acreage of exactly one acre.

MARIGOLD: Was it golden for you too?

DAD: You were golden.

MARIGOLD: Daddy, we've still got Paco's feathers in the bathroom. In that tall vase above the toilet. I used to collect them off the ground and put them in that vase.

DAD: It was in the parlor.

MARIGOLD: Grandma always called it the parlor.

DAD: On the pinewood table in the parlor. Now they're in the toilet.

MARIGOLD: Above the toilet.

DAD: Are they really still there? I haven't noticed them for years. How long do peacock feathers last do you suppose?

MARIGOLD: I don't know. A long time.

DAD: Why did you come home?

Pause.

Old Paco . . . He must've had a head like an anvil.

Pause.

When John was an infant . . .

Pause.

When your brother was an infant, I myself was no more than a terrified teenager. John, your oldest brother. My two friends would come over after work, and we'd sit around the place listening to rockabilly records and drinking beer and smoking reefer, baby-sitting little John. God knows what poor little John did—listened to records and drank beer and smoked pot, probly, just like we were doing. Then around ten at night your mom would come home from work, and we'd leave her with the baby and go down to this burger joint and take turns banging on the pinball machine . . . me and my friends. Ron Parker and Snooky Styles. The friends I knew when I was nineteen were the most important friends I ever had. Good Lord, that reefer. We got it from the Meskins. It was all over South Texas.

You could buy it by the stick for ten cents a piece. After we all left Texas I've never smoked it since. But it must've got in my blood and into you all, because my children certainly came out into this world with an unmanageable taste for contraband. (*Pause.*) Ron and Snooky and yours truly . . . we wanted to be poets and writers and cool cats.

Pause.

MARIGOLD: Well, I guess I better—

DAD: Don't leave me.

MARIGOLD: I won't.

DAD: Stay.

MARIGOLD: I'll stay.

DAD: Stay. Watch the TV with me.

MARIGOLD: Whatcha watchin'?

DAD: Who knows. Who can make sense of it these days . . .

He hits the mute.

TV: Huge establishing helicopter shot taking in several blocks of the South State Street area of Ukiah, California: three intersections, two shopping malls, the life of our moment . . . where a guy pushes a long train of shopping carts toward the Safeway and a team of tiny white-garbed Little

Leaguers trails out of the Taco Bell while two trucks crash at a corner and the two men driving get out and start to quarrel, one throwing the other up against his hood, and three hawks glide down out of the yellow hills and a fifth grader sets a fire in a trash can behind the movies and his two laughing friends douse it with their giant Cokes and our strange, strange captain sails us deeper down toward the unfathomable springs of the sea. THE END.

DAD: No. It's not the end . . .

Pause.
Lights dim as DAD *cries out:*

DAD: Sad! Beautiful! Beautiful! Sad!

BLACKOUT

Act II

SCENE 2

The downstairs as at the close of Act I. A couple of hours have passed.
A wedding.
    PASTOR ROCK *presides, bravely and tolerantly grinning whenever he gets the chance to.* GIB *and* SUZANNE *face him, standing hand in hand more or less in the kitchen.*
    GRANDMA *stands by the counter and stares.*
    BRO, *in the recliner, sits and smokes a Kool and stares. The Chihuahua dog looks on, too.*

PASTOR ROCK:

> Unto thee, O Lord, do I lift up my soul.
> O my God, I trust in thee: Let me not be ashamed,
> Let not mine enemies triumph over me.
> Yea, let none that wait on thee be ashamed:
> Let them be ashamed which transgress without cause.
> Remember, O Lord, thy tender mercies;
> For they have been ever of old.
> Remember not the sins of my youth,
> Nor my transgressions:
> According to thy mercy remember thou me for thy goodness's sake, O Lord.
> Good and upright is the Lord: Therefore will he teach sinners in the way.
> For thy name's sake, O Lord, pardon mine iniquity; for it is great.

Pause.

> What man is he that—

GIB: That's very good, Pastor Rock, that's quite excellent— I like that a great deal. Thank you.

SUZANNE: Thank you, Pastor.

PASTOR ROCK *notices* GRANDMA'*s revolver on the counter.*

PASTOR ROCK: Uh—

GIB: Suzanne, I vow to you—

PASTOR ROCK: Well, okay—uh. Is this loaded?

BRO: Off—and on.

GIB: —vow to be faithful and loving and kind. To lead you only when you ask me to, and to follow you when you know the way and I don't know the way. To be your husband forever, to have and to hold until death. (*Pause.*) Okay—

SUZANNE: Uh, Gib, Gilbert, I vow to you to be faithful and loving and kind. To lead—(*Dog is barking.*) Please, doggie, please! Shut up!—to lead only when you—damn it damn it damn it—

She kicks dog out of the front door.

Sorry, Mrs. Cassandra—

GRANDMA: Kick it to death. It ain't my dog.

PASTOR ROCK: I now pronounce you—oh:

SUZANNE: —to lead only when you ask me to, and to follow you when you know the way and I don't know the way. To be your wife forever, to have and to hold until death.

PASTOR ROCK: You may kiss the bride.

GIB. Wait—you didn't pronounce—

PASTOR ROCK: I mean okay, okay, okay. (*Chuckling desperately:*) I'm out here in the dead of night, remember. I now—which is rapidly turning out to be the crack of dawn—okay . . . uh . . .

Door to outside has begun thumping rhythmically. CASS's *voice scats to an old instrumental tune called "Tequila."*

CASS'S VOICE OUTSIDE:
> Ba-*bamp* ba-ba-*ba*-ba *bomp* bomp—
> Ba-*bamp* ba-ba-*ba*-ba *bomp*—
> Ba-*bamp* ba-ba-*ba*-ba *bomp* bomp—
> Ba-*bamp* ba-ba-*ba*-ba . . . *bomp*—

GRANDMA *opens the door.* CASS *enters with both hands full of groceries, still attempting to pound out a rhythm on the door with his head. The dog slips in, too.*

CASS: Grammaw, if you want a miracle I just met a man can turn dollar bills into tequila!

He sets out two fifths of Cuervo Gold and a lot of lemons, and gets a knife, salt, so on.

> Ba-*bamp* ba-ba-*ba*-ba *bomp* bomp—Watch it, doggie, watch it, doggie, watch it, doggie . . . Hola, compadres y muchachos! Back from the hanging!

GIB: Whose?

CASS: Yours.

GRANDMA: What do you think you're doing now?

CASS: In the family tradition, I am going to get "blotto." I warned you all. I told everybody I'd sacrifice one more lemon on the altar, the night before I go to the Starlight.

GRANDMA: But you won't go in tomorrow! It might be days!

CASS: Then I'll be drunk for days. LET THE LEMONS TREMBLE!

BRO: Jesus John F. Kennedy and Elvis, boy. You do make a party when you want to!

CASS: I do.

BRO: You light up the room with your mischievous grin!

With rapid skillful teamwork the two brothers slice lemons wholesale, pop open both fifths.

Toasting each present one by one—each brother drinking straight from his jug—subdued, reverent, very fast:

CASS AND BRO: Your health—
Your health—
Your health—
Yours—
Yours—
Your health—
This guy. This guy—
This guy's health—

Pause. CASS *takes in the scene.*

CASS: Was I interrupting something?

BRO: Up to now you haven't seen the real me. You've only been seeing me all nostalgic and wine-drunk. Now you'll see the real me.

He guzzles.

PASTOR ROCK: Uh . . . I think if you drink a whole fifth too rapidly, it'll kill you.

BRO: And what happens if you never ever touch the stuff? You die anyway.

CASS *pulls a smoke from a recently opened pack in his pocket. Shares with his brother.*

CASS (*yelling upstairs*): Dad! Would you like a Kool! I got one million of 'em here. Whoops! One million minus one!

CASS AND BRO (*together*): NINE HUNNERD 'N' NINETY-NINE THOUSAND, NINE HUNNERD 'N' NINETY-NINE.

GRANDMA (*to* BRO): It'll be just like last time. Only it'll be this time on *top* of last time, because they're still after you— and *John*—

BRO: Now, John has got some serious trouble. But my warrant is under a whole stack of other warrants by now.

CASS: I don't think your bonding agent's gonna just forget it though.

BRO: A thousand dollars. He's wrote it off by now, and it's slipped out of his memory . . . There shouldn't even be such a charge as "resisting arrest." Do they expect you to go willingly?

GRANDMA: You must pay your debt to the law.

BRO: *I* don't owe the—! Somebody owes *me* a tooth! Do you remember how I lost this tooth? That cop had his Thirty-eight Special shoved *all the way* inside my mouth. Some of these people are dangerous . . . Jesus Christ.

CASS: Jesus Christ indeed, sir.

GRANDMA: Cass, please. Don't take our Lord in vain. For your own sake.

CASS: I'm sorry. But weren't you the one kind of surprised me a while ago saying "ass"?

GRANDMA: "Ass" is acceptable speech now. They say it on TV. And "penis" too. I don't decide these things!

CASS *bangs for order with his fifth.*

CASS: Question! Got a question . . . Folks!

Pause.

What's the deal?

Pause.

PASTOR ROCK: Well, you've come to a sort of, a little—wedding ceremony, certainly a very *unusual*—

CASS: Did I miss it?

PASTOR ROCK: No . . . Not all of it.

CASS: Did I miss the part about speak now or forever, you know—

GIB: We're not doing that part.

SUZANNE: Well—

BRO: What am I supposed to say?

GIB: Jesus. Do you expect him to say something?

SUZANNE: Not necessarily—I just—

BRO: Ha! Acknowledgment! Uh—I'll have a double!

CASS *shoves both bottles at him.*

CASS: What's happening here, Brother Luke? Are you think-ing you're going to marry her? (*Toasting all:*) I do! I do!

BRO: No. I'll sit this one out. You two go ahead and get mar-ried. (*Raising his jug:*) I'll observe.

SUZANNE: He's got his true love.

DOG: Bark! bark bark bark!

SUZANNE (*kicking dog out and going right into kicking* BRO): Damn it damn it damn it—Luke!—Luke!—Luke!—

BRO: Bro.

SUZANNE: Bro! (*Pause.*) There's a brand-new, year-two-thousand SS Camaro outside that *we* pulled up in.

GIB: Zero to sixty in five seconds flat. Kind of puts a stop to all the speculation about "Are we there yet."

BRO: So it's all about the style to which you're accustomed.

SUZANNE: No. I'm *accustomed* to shoes from the thrift store with other women's dried-up foot-sweat in them. I'm accustomed to the ninety-nine-cent fast-food drive-thru special. I'm accustomed to eating burgers and tacos off my lap and listening to the one-speaker stereo and apartments with six-and-a-half-foot ceilings and cigarette scars on the linoleum and cigarette scars on the carpet and a puddle of oil under the car with the power window that won't roll up. I'm accustomed to taking my little book of food stamps to eight different checkout counters to buy eight packs of gum so I can get enough change in actual U.S. money to buy a half-rack of Tombstone Beer and a pack of no-name cigarettes with a fistful of quarters, pennies, nickels, and dimes. (*Pause.*) With you, my past becomes my future again . . . Because if I went back with you I'd just end up divorcing you like last time and marrying him like I'm doing now, so why don't I just marry him now and get it over with and save all that time? . . . Because it just gets slowly and slowly and slowly more obvious. You're a trauma case. A kidnapped child.

BRO: A what?

SUZANNE: A wolf boy.

BRO: *What?*

CASS: She's making sense.

BRO: To who? . . . Aaaaah. You're *all* on a self-help . . . *thing*.

SUZANNE: I know a wolf boy when I see one.

BRO: You read a scientific book. Your ricochet rebop!

SUZANNE: Your trauma stopped you at the age of nine. You're stalled halfway inside the human race. Half of you is outside. Like a wolf boy. There's a lot of you you can't talk about. You just howl and bite. I wasn't going to stay married to that kind of stuff.

BRO: Your ripoff repartee!

SUZANNE: A kidnapped child. You're looking for somebody to ransom you. But I'm marrying Gib.

CASS (*to his jug*): I do! I do! (*Drinks. Lays his head on the counter. Meanwhile:*)

BRO: *Be* that . . . as it may. *He* . . . loves my sister. He is eternally in love with Marigold. Since he was six . . . I was there. At the pool. He took one look at her and dunked her till she had to be rescued. Took one look at her, and he just had to drown her. That's a very common expression of love.

GIB: No.

BRO: One particular form of love. "I love you so much I have to kill you." That kind.

SUZANNE: The pool?

BRO: Down over there at the Earl Warren Civic Pool the second day after we moved here from Texas.

SUZANNE: The pool?

GIB: They renamed that pool. It's the Harvey Milk Recreation Center now. Everybody calls it the Milk Pool of course.

BRO: Two people . . . Listen, it doesn't matter—all the vows, you know, you know, young people, youngsters like we were, me and Suzanne, and you and Marigold, the eternal pledges we made in the backseat over on River Road, okay, all right, because that was, the majority of it, hormones and sex: we admit it don't none of it matter. *But—*

GIB: Suzanne, I don't remember anything like this. (*To* BRO:) You know what your trouble is? You haven't evolved beyond the reptile part of your moral development. You're like the scorpion who stings the frog even though they both drown. You'll lie when the truth will save you. I say this as a friend.

BRO: The scorpion is an insect.

GIB: Do you know the fable about the scorpion and the frog?

BRO: Well, which am I? A reptile or an insect?

GIB: The frog carries the scorpion across the river—

SUZANNE: —but the scorpion can't help himself, he's such an insect he stings the frog to death even though it causes his own death—

GIB:—by drowning.

BRO: Like you wanted to drown my sister. The minute you fell in love.

GIB: He's twisting everything. I won't touch your shit, Luke.

GRANDMA: You can't debate somebody with an insane mentality. Leave him alone.

GIB: Whether he's crazy or not, Mrs. Cassandra—the point is that he lies.

BRO: What facts have I made up? Which facts out of what I said are falsehoods?

GIB: You're putting a wild misinterpretation on everything you say. I don't have a thing for your sister. That's history so ancient I—well, I'm not in your fantasy universe. There's nobody in it but you.

BRO: Oh yeah? I got a surprise for you. Sis—come on down! (*He goes to hallway.*) Sis! Sister Marigold! I'm gonna keep yelling till I'm hoarse or till you make an appearance at this glorious feast! You, are, invited, to, a wedding!

Pause. Footsteps come slowly down. All watch the entrance to hallway. MARIGOLD *appears at the border of the room, taking in the scene but not entering. Meanwhile:*

TV: It's time now for the Jerry Springer show! This week—the rotten corpse of dead love rises up and speaks English. Tambien en Español.

GIB: You shut up.

BRO: Damn right—I already *shot* you *once*—

BRO *draws his sister one step into the room.*

Now tell him who is the love of your life. Tell him, Sis.

MARIGOLD: . . . Wow. Did you create this scene?

BRO: Several points are being driven home all at once. He's making his, and I'm making mine—which is: You've never even looked at another man, besides this fool.

MARIGOLD: As far as you know.

BRO: Okay . . .

MARIGOLD: But please notice I'm not blind, Bro. So—I've looked. What I'm in need of is an orphan. Or a guy with just one tiny old widowed mom in San Diego who plays cards all day long in the Home and can't even recollect her children's names.

GRANDMA: Oh! Lord!

MARIGOLD: Grandma, all I'm saying is I've got all the family one person can handle.

GRANDMA: All anybody could stand.

MARIGOLD: You're all I want.

BRO: Aaaaaaah—

MARIGOLD: And Gib and I—I don't know—

GIB: Childhood sweethearts.

MARIGOLD: Childhood sweethearts.

GIB: Childhood's over. For quite a few of us. *Some*—are stuck.

BRO: Aw dry up and quit stinkin'.

GIB: Okay! . . . (*To* MARIGOLD:) Yeah, you were special to me. And while we were going together, I was very happy. But then I went in the service and—sure. I'm different, you're different, we're all . . . *different*. But somehow you—inside of you, you stayed all . . . the *same*.

BRO: That's why he just had to drown you.

MARIGOLD: Drown me? I don't remember ever drowning.

BRO: Of course you don't remember. Of course you don't remember. But you drowned. You drowned and you never came up.

BRO *sits in the recliner and cuddles with his jug.*

MARIGOLD: Now will somebody please explain to me about John?

PASTOR ROCK: Can't we get on with the—?

GRANDMA: John's in jail in Texas! They caught him up north and dragged him down to Dallas on a bus.

PASTOR ROCK: We've got to make some headway here—

MARIGOLD: A bus?

GRANDMA: This bus . . . *zigzags* the country letting prisoners on and prisoners off. Every third day they stop for one eight-hour rest stop to let them sleep inside the walls of a prison they never saw before or heard of before. They travel otherwise on their bus, chained together by one long chain snaking along through their shackles. Like slaves in Cecil B. DeMille. Only, the prisoners of today never rise up in rebellion, because they get cereal every morning spiked full of tranquilizing dope. But do you want to know who the dope is? *I'll* tell you who the dope is: Cecil B. DeMille! He's got no idea how we live! We zigzag up and down the national highways with our eyeballs as glazed as candy, chained together and drooling spit! And what was poor John's crime to begin it all? Drinking and driving! Then they chased him, and life got exciting! Putting him in prison is the utter waste of a good mind! All the Cassandras have pretty good minds! Maybe they don't care to take them out and dust them off and *use* them, but . . . (*pointing at* BRO:) *There's* the one to be locked up as soon as possible!

GIB *turns his back on* MARIGOLD. *Takes* SUZANNE'*s hand. They face* PASTOR ROCK.

Pause.

CASS *passed out at the kitchen counter . . .* BRO *stupefied by drink and looking on, slumped in the recliner . . .* GRANDMA *and* MARIGOLD *standing aside, steeped in hesitation . . . Lights dim. The* PASTOR *reads in a hushed and momentarily holy atmosphere . . .*

PASTOR ROCK:
　　Remember, O Lord, thy tender mercies and thy loving-kindnesses;
　　For they have been ever of old.
　　Remember not the sins of my youth,
　　Nor my transgressions:
　　According to thy mercy remember thou me for thy goodness's sake, O Lord.
　　Good and upright is the Lord: Therefore will he teach sinners in the way.
　　The meek will he guide in judgment: and the meek will he teach his way.
　　All the paths of the Lord are mercy and truth unto such as keep his covenant and his testimonies.

For thy name's sake, O Lord, pardon mine iniquity; for it is great.

... I now pronounce you husband and wife.

Lights come up as:

GIB: I may now kiss the bride?

PASTOR ROCK: Buddy, you can do whatever you want to her. (*Apologetic:*) Just let me get on home to my own darn wife. Here now. Sign this. This is what counts.

BRO: You just married the wrong people to the wrong people.

BRO *eases himself down onto the floor. Meanwhile* GIB *and* SUZANNE *sign the marriage certificate:*

BRO: Good night ...

PASTOR ROCK: Just here.

BRO: The entire universe can kiss my ass ...

PASTOR ROCK: Now the Mrs. Yes ...

BRO: We a long way from Hell. But I can still smell the smoke ...

Meanwhile, MARIGOLD *enters fully and looks down on* BRO *and nudges him with her toe, then* CASS.

MARIGOLD (*to* CASS): Long time no see. Hi, Cass!

CASS (*head down, immobile*): Sis. Sis. Good old Sis. Sis.

MARIGOLD: Congratulations, lovebirds.

GRANDMA: Many happy returns! . . . No. That's not what I
mean . . .

GIB AND SUZANNE: Thank you, thanks. Thank you.

About to leave, PASTOR ROCK *opens the door and quickly slams it
shut.*

PASTOR ROCK: Uh-oh.

SUZANNE: What did you see there?

PASTOR ROCK (*shaken*): I open the door and all I see is—
midair. Nothing to stand on. It's like a cartoon.

BRO (*on the floor*): Oh yeah!

PASTOR ROCK: And everything's all shimmery, like a mirage.
You can see right through the cars.

GRANDMA: And it's colored all funny, like silk.

PASTOR ROCK: Yeah. Yes, ma'am . . . Who told you?

GRANDMA: It's like that every day. It's the sunrise.

PASTOR ROCK: And there were angels or eagles or—coming
down from the sky. Huge creatures with wings.

GRANDMA: That's just crows.

MARIGOLD: Sometimes. Or gulls.

PASTOR ROCK: With a ten-foot wingspan?

MARIGOLD: Magnified sort of by the sunrise and thermals and mist and all—like a lens.

The PASTOR *cracks the door, slams it shut, blinded.*

PASTOR ROCK: Let me get this straight. Every day about this time you can open your door and see the whole world changed into another planet?

GRANDMA: Almost. Nine days out of ten I'd say.

PASTOR ROCK: Wow. What do you pay for rent?

GRANDMA. It's government subsidized.

PASTOR ROCK: I just meant it'd be extra, you'd think.

BRO (*on the floor*): I wouldn't pay one dime extra for midair and mirages.

PASTOR ROCK: Well, all right! "What man is he that feareth the Lord? Him shall he teach in the way that he shall choose."

He dons a pair of sunglasses from his pocket. Opens the door, cringing against the light outside. Holds out his hand behind him:

PASTOR ROCK: Who's with me?

GIB *and* SUZANNE *and the* PASTOR, *hand in hand, make an exit, all blinded by the light.*

PASTOR ROCK: On into tomorrow!

Lights dim. By low illumination, players move slowly into position for Scene 3.

Act II

SCENE 3

Lights up on the downstairs. Two hours later. GRANDMA *and* MARIGOLD *at the dining table,* BRO *in the recliner unconscious,* CASS *passed out on the floor.*
    Front door still open, light streaming in.
    TV *sings a Heartache Song:*

TV:
    All your promises, the things you said,
    Using grand words like eternity and love.

    You told me together we would see the end of time.
    You told me together we would watch the last star fall.

    The horrible thing is you meant it.
    The awful truth is you meant every word.

    My heart breaks for anybody saying those words tonight.
    My heart breaks for anybody listening.

GRANDMA *stares outside dreamily as the music plays. The song ends. She stares harder and harder at something outdoors.*

GRANDMA: Lord, look at this coming. Oh my Lord, she's shining in the sunlight.

MARIGOLD *too stares in wonder.*
    MARCY *enters slowly.*
    A big girl in a peasant blouse and tie-dyed floor-length skirt hung with innumerable tiny mirrors. Made up spectacularly like the goddess of death, Kali: black hair with fake jewels in it and sequins and absolutely all that stuff.
    Her skin is dyed bright blue and her eyeshadow is red and her mascara is silver and gold.
    She paces very carefully forward.
    Bells dangle from the hem of her glittering skirt. She moves slowly, as if trying not to ring them, but rings them anyhow with a slight bump and grind at the end of each pace.
    She carries a drawstring purse as if it were something quite special. She wears well-used farm-type work shoes.
    She stops before the television.

MARCY: Wow. Uh-oh. Your TV isn't going to work unless you fix it.

TV: Ass! Penis! Penis! Ass!

MARCY: It works a little bit, though. That's something, at least.

TV: I'm down, but I'm not out!

MARCY *takes a seat in a stray dining chair in the center of the room.*

Pause.

GRANDMA: What are you so smug about, young lady? What's got you sitting there like the queen of I don't know what?

MARCY: Don't you see me?

GRANDMA: I see you gloried up like a Hindu. In danger of setting a fire with yourself just sitting there. (*Pause.*) Who are you?

MARCY: Marcy.

Pause.

I'm really just Marcy.

GRANDMA: Marcy who? (*Pause.*) Are you with the Social Services?

MARCY: No. I've seen them though. I've talked to them. A lot.

GRANDMA: I believe you have. I would think you'd have a great deal to say to each other. Where'd you come from?

MARCY: I came from Redding . . . I bought this dress and got a spiritual makeover. Her name was Jasmine Daylight. I got it from Jasmine Daylight. A makeover to bring out my beautiful spirit and let it dance. And a dress for my beautiful spirit to dance in. But it's hot. Because I still have my jeans on underneath. (*Pause.*) Bro is asleep, it looks like.

Pause while they all look at BRO *asleep.*

GRANDMA: Redding!

MARCY: At the Fantasia Fair. It cost all my money, but it was sure worth it.

Pause.

GRANDMA: How did you find this place?

MARCY: Robert knew where it was. I showed him my notepad. (*Opening the drawstring purse:*) It's got the address and phone number of every person I've ever met. If they would like to give it to me. Not everybody likes to give you their address and their phone number. (*Hands the notebook to* GRANDMA.)

GRANDMA: What on earth do you mean for me to do with this? I don't need to call anybody.

MARCY: Would you like to give me yours? Your address and your phone number?

GRANDMA: Well it must be *in* here, for you to *be* here. Or else you just exploded from a magic hat out in the front yard. Good Lord. I've never seen anything like you. Where'd you get my address? I never gave it to you. I wouldn't do that. You might visit me. (*Reading a page:*) It's the last one in here.

MARCY: This is Bro's home address. Right? His full name is Luke Cassandra.

GRANDMA: Luke! Did Luke give out this address?

MARCY: He gave it to me.

GRANDMA: When?

MARCY: When he left.

GRANDMA: Left where?

MARCY: Where we live. The land. I own it.

Pause. GRANDMA *looks* MARCY *over, sniffing.*

GRANDMA: You smell kind of nice. I might as well compliment you on that much.

MARCY: You know what's making me smell like this? It's called spikenard. Ointment of spikenard from the Fantasia Fair. I think it smells like different spices. What do you think it smells like?

GRANDMA: Whatever you want to say it does. That's fine with me.

MARCY: Spices it is, then. Spices. Well, well! Here comes a little dog. Whose little dog are you?

GRANDMA: Shoo! *Shoo! She* don't know whose dog she is. Bro! Wake up now. Look alive. Bro!

BRO *wakes up in the recliner and sees* MARCY *bending to pet the little dog.*

He finds a smoke and lights it.
Pause.

BRO: Jesus Christ.

MARCY: Hi, Bro. Is this your little dog? (BRO *just stares.*) Or whose dog is it? (*To* MARIGOLD:) Your dog?

MARIGOLD: No . . . Nope . . .

BRO: Jesus H. Elvis Presley goddamn Christ.

MARCY: I was at the Fantasia Fair. Then I said where you were and a man gave me a ride.

BRO: All the way from Redding?

MARCY: Yes. From the Fantasia Fair.

BRO: A man?

MARCY: A man at the Fantasia Fair.

BRO: Jesus Christ.

MARCY: No . . . His name was Robert Aiken.

BRO: I bet he was achin'. What'd he do to you?

MARCY: He gave me a ride. From the Fantasia Fair.

BRO: Jesus Christ.

GRANDMA: Jesus Christ Jesus Christ Jesus Christ. With you it's always somebody's name in vain or you can't be satisfied! (*To* MARCY:) What do you want, darlin'?

MARCY: Nothing.

GRANDMA: Are you hungry? Did you eat?

MARCY: Can I have some of the popcorn?

Still speechless, MARIGOLD *fetches the popcorn.* MARCY *eats daintily, one kernel at a time. They watch.* BRO *in particular watches, fascinated.*

GRANDMA: Marcy, is there any service we can do for you here?

MARCY: No thank you. Not right now. (*To* BRO:) I just want to go back to the land now. Is it okay?

BRO: Fine.

MARCY: In the Cadillac?

BRO: Marcy. What on earth are you talking about, Marcy?

MARCY: You said you were going to get a Cadillac.

BRO *rises, heads for the sink, tosses his cigarette into it, washes his face . . . chuckling sarcastically all the while.*

BRO: I know you're stupid, but can't you at least see this much about the situation? I can't go back.

MARCY: Well, can't you drive back in the Cadillac?

BRO: Marcy, I don't have the Cadillac yet. They cost money. I don't have money. I meant I'd get a life—get a job, get back to where I was, a place, my old honey Suzu, and someday get a Cadillac. None of this actually involved you.

MARCY: Do you have enough gas?

Pointing at MARCY, BRO *addresses the others.*

BRO: I left because of that reason.

MARCY: What reason? What reason?

BRO: Whatchamacallit, hell, you know goddamn it! . . . You can't talk to somebody who can only think one thought at a time. Believe me, trust me on this, I've made a very careful study of human thought processes. I should write a book. But nobody'd believe me.

The dog's at his feet.

DOG: Bark bark! bark bark bark!

BRO (*to dog*): I do not have time to get around and play! Goddamn it now! DOESN'T ANYBODY SENSE THAT?

Silence. CASS *wakes; moaning, moaning, moaning . . . struggles to his knees. Stares bleary-eyed at* MARCY.

MARCY: You woke up.

CASS: I don't exactly know about that.

CASS *crawls to the kitchen sink. Climbs upright, drinks and drinks at the tap. Splashes his face, turns around—looks at* MARCY. *Splashes again. Staggers over to the recliner. Sits himself. Rubs his face. Looks. Rubs his face. Stares. Pause.*

MARCY: You're awake.

CASS: If you say so. But I think an apparition like you would say just about anything. Boy. Ain't you something? You are something. Wow.

MARCY: I had a spiritual makeover at the Fantasia Fair.

CASS: Did you? I got no idea what those words could possibly ever mean. Does anybody know what those words are supposed to mean? (*Rifling his shirt pocket.*) I got one two three four cigarettes. Who's got a light . . .

MARCY: Could we go back pretty soon, Bro?

Pause. CASS *stares afresh at* MARCY.

CASS: Is this—? . . . Wow. Fantastic! . . . Are you the one living with Bro? Or he's living with you, I mean? Is that who you are?

MARCY: We live on the land I own. He lives there and I live there. That's who I am.

CASS: You got here all on your own? All the way from Redding?

MARCY (*delighted*): I have to tell everybody everything every time!

CASS: Oh—sorry . . .

MARCY: That's okay. I'm getting pretty good at it!

CASS: I don't think you're retarded at all.

MARCY: Thank you.

GRANDMA: You've been living with him how long exactly?

MARCY: A pretty long time.

GRANDMA: Well, how long more or less?

Pause while MARCY *considers.*

BRO: Aaaaah . . . Since more or less right after I jumped bail, and what does that do for ya? That pretty much put the horns and the goatee on your grandson? And the little spike tail on my butt?

MARCY: The animals must be missing us.

BRO: Is anybody there? Who's tending the stock?

MARCY: They're waiting.

BRO: Good God. When he gets hungry enough the burro's gonna kick out the fence boards and go get in the grain sack, and the dogs are gonna chase him around till he busts one of 'em's *head* off with a good swift kick, and your precious nanny goat's probably dead by now of thirst, and her kids are starving.

MARCY: I filled the tank, Bro. And all the troughs and all the bowls for the dogs.

BRO: You got two little kids pulling and sucking at the dead dried-up jugs of their mother.

Pause.

(*To* MARIGOLD:) Can I ask what you think you're looking at?

MARIGOLD: Nothing.

BRO: You never said so much as hi.

MARIGOLD: Hi hi hi, Bro. Howdy do. Actually I kicked you in the butt a little while ago. Right in your spiky tail. But you know what? You were blissfully indisposed. And hello to you, too, Marcy. You're a dazzling sight.

MARCY: Thank you.

MARIGOLD: You're welcome.

BRO (*to* MARIGOLD): You were always the bright and airy one.

CASS: Actually, that ain't her fault, Bro.

BRO: Are you gonna jump up and down on me now, too?

CASS: No. I'm just telling somebody something. (*To* MARIGOLD:) Sis, you don't remember. You never got touched by one breath of any of this. Any of our business . . . You're our angel of the family. And I mean that respectfully. I mean no sarcasm, Sis.

BRO: Of course you don't remember. You'd forget World War Two. And Vietnam. You wouldn't remember Hiroshima if it happened up yer butt. Your mind is one big candy cloud.

MARIGOLD: It's true. I don't remember any tragedies. No Texas, no Momma, no vehicular homicide. I just remember growing up in Ukiah with sweet friends in school and three interesting crazy older brothers and a dad and a grandma who spoiled me. In a big old house with a big old dusty yard full of chickens. (*Mainly to* MARCY:) All you have to be is tiny and innocent enough, and the worst storm just blows right past you.

BRO: Momma was the storm, and the storm ran right over us—especially over Amy, and it killed her. And Amy was more innocent than you'll ever be.

GRANDMA: And quite a bit tinier. She wasn't four months old I believe.

CASS: If I had a light . . .

BRO *yanks the cigarette from* CASS's *fingers. Turns with it to* MARCY.

BRO: Here. Have a delicious Kool. (*She takes it.*) Put it in your mouth.

MARCY: I don't smoke . . . I'm not oral.

BRO: Then what are you? Anal? . . . Dangle it between your lips and turn sideways. I'm gonna shoot it out of your mouth.

He grabs the pistol off the counter, and a bullet, too.

GRANDMA (*quietly—almost reverently*): I'd say there's been enough silly madness for one night around here. For a lifetime . . . But nobody listens . . .

Meanwhile, BRO shoves the bullet into the cylinder, snaps it closed with a flick of the wrist, and gestures that MARCY should turn sideways.
    MARCY sighs and turns her profile. She puts the cigarette between her lips.
    BRO sights down the pistol, not three feet away from her. Cocks back the hammer.
    The barrel of the gun begins to jiggle. He repositions his shooting arm, holding the weapon with both hands.

BRO: Stand still. Real still. Don't move. Shut your eyes.

As he speaks, he moves closer. Closer. Until the mouth of the gun is right against the cigarette in MARCY's mouth. She shuts her eyes.
    Pause.

CASS (*very quietly*): Don't do it.

BRO (*very calmly*): Are we gonna have it out now?

CASS (*very softly*): Have what out, Bro? What have we got against each other? What have you got against anybody here?

BRO (*also softly*): I don't know. I wish I could put my finger on it.

GRANDMA: You were such a beautiful, beautiful boy!

Pause.
    He strikes MARCY *about the head—three quick blows with the gun.*

BRO: BAM! BAM! BAM! YEAH.

MARCY *cries out, collapses.*
    Pause.
    BRO *dangles the gun by two fingers above her weeping form. Then drops it.*

GRANDMA: Get away from there! Leave her be!

BRO *retrieves the Kool, steps back, and observes while* MARIGOLD, CASS, *and* GRANDMA *get* MARCY *into the recliner. He lights up and smokes. Meanwhile, overlapping:*

MARIGOLD: There. That's good now. I'll get a cloth—

CASS: God oh God oh God. Okay. Okay now—

MARCY: Ow. Ow. Ow. I have to spit. I have to spit. There's blood inside my mouth.

GRANDMA: You'll be—we'll get you—are you hurt bad? How bad is she hurt—get a cloth!—she is *bleeding*!—a cold cloth!

MARIGOLD *gets a cloth wet at the sink and returns to the others to wipe gently at* MARCY'*s face.*

MARIGOLD: Just spit in the cloth if you need to, Marcy, hon. I'll get another one.

MARCY (*snuffing and spitting*): My whole mouth hurts. And my whole face. My *ear* hurts, Bro.

BRO (*to* MARIGOLD): There you go, Sis. Right? Huh? Her ear hurts and her whole face hurts. Huh?

GRANDMA *and* MARIGOLD *minister to the patient. Meanwhile:*

CASS: Nice. Nice . . . Nice going, Bro. I think you broke her nose.

BRO (*to* MARIGOLD): And it looks like her nose is broke.

MARCY: What do you mean?

GRANDMA: Honey. Oh hon. Honey now. Nothing.

MARCY: What happens if my nose is broken?

GRANDMA: Nothing. They'll fix it. They know how to fix your nose if it's broken.

CASS *stands up straight. Sighs. Looks his brother over. Turns and exits toward the stairs. We hear his footsteps going up.*
     Everybody looks up, following the sound of his ascent, until all is quiet again.

BRO *approaches* MARCY. MARIGOLD *and* GRANDMA *step back involuntarily. He kneels before her. She's crying without a sound.*
Pause.
He speaks to her very softly.

BRO: Hi . . .

MARCY: Hi . . .

BRO: What are you doing?

MARCY: Nothing . . . Just thinking . . .

BRO: About what?

MARCY: About my birthday.

Pause.

BRO: Yeah?

MARCY: There was a rainbow on my birthday.

GRANDMA *weeps. Bawls. Wails . . .*

BRO: Now what?

GRANDMA: You'll never know more of Jesus Christ than that
    right there!

Pause.

BRO: Yeah . . . Yeah . . . Her nose is broke, Sis. There. I rest my case.

Pause.

MARIGOLD: I don't know what to say about that. Maybe I was wrong. Maybe it's random torture. From here to Pluto and beyond. I don't know . . . Where have you *been*? What *happened* to you when you were *there*?

BRO: Well, Sis, I don't think I've got time to tell you about it. Not right now . . . But when I do, get out your tape recorder . . . Because it's quite a story, and then some . . .

Lights fade to black downstairs as lights come up dim on the upper bedroom. CASS *lies side by side with* DAD, *the two of them watching* TV *together, bathed in its steel-blue light.*

BRO'S VOICE: The story of a bail-jumping fugitive crossing the Trinity Alps on foot by cover of darkness with the bounty-hunter vigilantes on his trail, holing up in caves during the day, stealing pies off windowsills to feed his withering famished skeleton—and stumbling down the east side of the mountains and onto the farmstead of a helpless child-woman, a goddamn retard, and I wind up taking unfair advantage of her in every possible way for a half of a decade. Oh yeah, be there for that one . . .

Pinpoint spots pick up three figures downstairs: GRANDMA *in the kitchen;* MARIGOLD *at the counter;* MARCY *sitting up straight, glittering and eerie.*

Upstairs, DAD *and* CASS *watch the tube: as if the story we hear were televised.*

BRO'S VOICE: I'm just one of these ghosts tumbling through town. Old placers and Spaniard padres and destroyers of the noble redwoods. Okies and Arkies and wetbacks and hippies and hobos. We just blow along through your town like dandelion chaff. Sumbitches got no use for us . . . Ghosts of the pioneers.

BLACKOUT

Perennial

Books by Denis Johnson:

SHOPPERS: *Two Plays*

ISBN 0-06-093440-9 (Trade paperback original available May 2002)

The noted poet, novelest and reporter takes a different direction with two new plays: *Shoppers Carried by Escalators Into the Flames*, and *Hellhound on My Trail*—dark stories with a unique cast of characters.

"He's simply one of the few writers around whose sentences make you shudder."—Adrienne Miller, *Esquire Review*

ANGELS

ISBN 0-06-098882-7 (Available in paperback May 2002)

Johnson's first novel (about two born losers) is now back in print.

"A terrifying book, a mixture of poetry and obscenity ... [the characters] are people who can't be ignored."—*New York Times Book Review*

SEEK: *Reports from the Edges of America and Beyond*

ISBN 0-06-093047-0 (paperback)

Representing the best of Johnson's reporting over the past twenty years, *Seek* introduces a cast of characters and brand of Americans most of us never meet, and takes us to a place where most reporters do not venture.

"Conjures up a world that is as tangible as it is magical."
— *Philadelphia Inquirer*

ALREADY DEAD: *A California Gothic*

ISBN 0-06-092909-X (paperback)

The disenfranchised scion to a northern California land fortune finds his future in a potentially profitable marijuana patch hidden on the family land.

"Denis Johnson . . . possess[es] a visionary sensibility [and] appreciation of the territory of the human soul." — *Newsday*

FISKADORO: *A Novel*

ISBN 0-06-097609-8 (paperback)

After nuclear war ravages their land, survivors must collect remnants of the old-world and rebuild their culture.

"Haunting . . . an eerie and powerful visionary novel." — *Boston Globe*

Available wherever books are sold, or call 1-800-331-3761 to order.

![Perennial logo] **Perennial**

JESUS' SON: *Stories by Denis Johnson*
ISBN 0-06-097577-6 (paperback)

An intense collection of interconnected stories that portray life through the eyes of a young man in a small Iowa town.

"Denis Johnson's most accessible and accomplished book, from start to finish, without a single sentence that misses the mark." — *Los Angeles Times*

THE NAME OF THE WORLD: *A Novel*
ISBN 0-06-092965-0 (paperback)

Facing the end of his stint at a small university Michael Reed finds himself forced "to act like somebody who cares what happens to him" for the fist time since the loss of his wife and child.

"A riveting read: wry, intense, exquisitely written." — *Entertainment Weekly*

RESUSCITATION OF A HANGED MAN: *A Novel*
ISBN 0-06-093466-2 (paperback)

The story of a detective's quest for love and redemption during a desolate winter in Provincetown.

"A cosmically charged fiction that combines hard-boiled theology and a redeeming wit — the perfect spiritual tonic." — *Kirkus Reviews*

THE STARS AT NOON: *A Novel*
ISBN 0-06-097610-1 (paperback)

A story of passion, fear, and betrayal told in the voice of an American woman whose mission in Central America is as shadowy as her surroundings.

"A daring novel . . . Denis Johnson is one of our most inventive, unpredictable novelists." — *New York Times Book Review*

THE THRONE OF THE THIRD HEAVEN OF THE NATIONS MILLENNIUM GENERAL ASSEMBLY: *Poems Collected and New*
ISBN 0-06-092696-1 (paperback)

Poems of grief and regret, of nightmare and acceptance, of redemption and the possibility of grace that present a vision of an American landscape.

"Denis Johnson's poems are driven by a ravening desire to make sense out of the life lived." — Raymond Carver

Available wherever books are sold, or call 1-800-331-3761 to order.